Tobias Schneebaum was born on the Lower East Side of Manhattan but spent most of his youth in Brooklyn. During World War II he served in the Army as a radar mechanic, and after the war studied art under Tamayo. He has been a painter ever since. At Tamayo's suggestion, he went to Mexico for three and a half years, where he painted and taught. In 1955 he was granted a Fulbright Fellowship to study painting in Peru, and it was during this time that he experienced the events described in this book.

After his return from South America, he had a one-man show in 1957 at the Peridot Gallery, where he has continued to show ever since. During the past decade he has traveled widely throughout Europe, Asia, and Africa, always alone, always choosing the back roads, away from civilization.

Keep The River On Your Right

by
Tobias
Schneebaum

Grove Press, Inc., New York

to Mary Britton Miller

"Look at every path closely and deliberately. Try it as many times as you think necessary. Then ask yourself, and yourself alone, one question. This question is one that only a very old man asks. My benefactor told me about it once when I was young, and my blood was too vigorous for me to understand it. Now I do understand it. I will tell you what it is: Does this path have a heart? All paths are the same: they lead nowhere. They are paths going through the bush, or into the bush. In my own life I could say I have traversed long, long paths, but I am not anywhere. My benefactor's question has meaning now. Does this path have a heart? If it does, the path is good; if it doesn't, it is of no use. Both paths lead nowhere; but one has a heart, the other doesn't. One makes for a joyful journey; as long as you follow it, you are one with it. The other will make you curse your life. One makes you strong; the other weakens you."

Don Juan,
Quoted in *The Teachings of Don Juan*
by Carlos Castaneda

Author's Note

In 1955 I went to Peru on a Fulbright fellowship and spent the latter part of my time there deep in the jungle among the people described in this book. I was away from civilization for such a long time that the U.S. embassy concluded that I had been killed, and there were announcements in the Peruvian newspapers and on the radio to that effect. Although I kept notes at the time, it has taken me all these years to come to the actual writing of the pages that follow. A considerable number of photographs of the Indians was presented to the National Geographic Society, in Washington, and other ethnographic materials to the American Museum of Natural History, in New York, when I first returned from Peru. Though I have altered time sequences in some places for narrative reasons, this story is based on what I witnessed, heard, and lived through. The names of the white people have been changed, as well as the names of the tribes themselves, and of the few places that would pinpoint the mission.

This book is not an attempt at an anthropological account of a tribe, but a record of my own becoming.

Keep
The River
On Your
Right

1

Manolo came into the clearing below me a little while ago, carrying in the crook of an elbow a basket of tomatoes he had gathered for supper. Little Chako, naked, followed him like a puppy wagging its tail, waving in his right hand the miniature bow and arrows that Manolo had made for him yesterday. Manolo went directly toward the kitchen to leave his basket, while Chako ran down the narrow beach and into the river, where the intestines of a tapir floated around Patiachi's legs. Chako grabbed at the long intestine and ran with it downstream as if it were a piece of string, then returned to splash around Patiachi, who paid no attention to him. Chako opened one end of the intestine and let the rushing water pour through it, washing the waste downstream. Patiachi had been cutting the body of the tapir into small pieces, wrapping the pieces in succulent leaves, then stuffing them for storage into sections of bamboo. Wassen, the ancient Topueri who had arrived here at the mission yesterday morning, hobbled like some prehistoric man to the water's edge, picked up the severed head of the tapir, and, with its blood dripping down his stomach and legs, wandered into the group of banana trees that hides the hut in which he is staying. Before disappearing behind the leaves, he turned to look at me, his eyes almost blank, his mouth a firm straight line surrounded by the six quivering, brilliant macaw feathers set into his flesh.

These are the only people visible as I sit here this afternoon to begin writing. I had lain awake through most of last night with thoughts of what I must put down. Ideas ran around my brain, and I tried to form the phrases through which I could convey exactly what had been happening within me while I was out there in the jungle all alone on my way here. It is difficult, almost impossible it seems to me now, to put it all into words that are meaningful. I will skip over what seems to me non-essential: the truck ride down from the top of the Andes, extraordinary as it was; the hotel at the end of the line, amusing as it was; the people I spoke to, strange and charming as they were; all are vague to me now, are part of a world that I have chosen to reject, to leave behind, as if my life began again the moment I started off in this direction.

This mission, where I now sit and write, is a place I had heard of from an archeologist, up in the mountains, with whom I had stayed some days. He had taken me around to Incaic ruins he himself had discovered, so that I could make drawings of them for him, and then had sent me to the Father Superior of the Escuela Santa Gloria, in Cuzco, who kept saying to me, "Just follow the river, just follow the river, you can't miss it. It's very easy. Just keep the river on your right." He himself had never been to the mission.

The hotel, at the very end of the dirt road in the little town of Pasñiquti, was a combination convalescent home, bordello and pension for the men who worked in the haciendas in the area. It was a noisy, cheerful place—so crowded, the night I arrived, that it was hours before I had a chance to talk to the owner. He laughed at me.

"You'll die. You'll be killed!" he said. "No one has ever gone there alone. No gun? No machete? You are crazy!"

He tried again in the morning to dissuade me, and he looked sad and bewildered as he gave me some dehydrated farina.

"Keep as close to the river as you can. You will lose it sometimes, because there is no beach for long sections, and the water will be deep. It will take you four, five, six days, maybe longer. I only went once myself, many years ago, with the padre himself and six Indians. No one has gone that way in many months. You are mad."

Climb a mountain. Enter a jungle. Cross the empty quarter of Arabia. Why? Sitting here a month later, healthy and happy, still excited, I can ask that question—why? Yet all I can do is ask it, for I have no answer. It never seemed possible that anything could happen to me. Somewhere, in another lifetime, I once read that the jungle either accepts you or rejects you. Did it accept me? or did I accept it? Does it matter? I walked on thinking only that I was on my way, to something.

The trail began several feet behind the hotel, just across a rope bridge that bounced and swayed with each step. It was a clear, well-traveled trail for the first couple of hours, and ran along the side of a hill. The trail was there for no reason that I could see. It ended at a cliff, high above the river: my guide. I slid down over loose earth, holding on to roots and bushes that helped slow my descent. Almost before I knew what was happening, thorned bamboo had caught at my clothes, thistled plants and tree trunks had left splinters in my hands, twigs had come out at me to scratch my face.

At the bottom of the cliff was a beach. That looked better right away. There were two white herons standing in shallow water. The sun was warm and pleasant as I began to walk over the small stones that almost completely hid the sand. Soon the stones seemed like giant rocks and I tripped over them. The sunlight on the river dazzled me and every minute took longer to go by. At times the beach disappeared, and I crossed hip-deep water to get to the other side. I came to the abandoned hut that had been described to me as the place to enter the jungle. It was some minutes before I found the trail. Reeds that had been cleanly cut with a machete showed me, finally, where the opening was, and into the mass of foliage I went.

The air was cool, and it took me several seconds to become accustomed to the darkness. Then I stood staring into a world of green. This was no forest to swing through at the end of a vine.

The trail itself was a tunnel through a solid mass of wild growth. Reed, cane, and paca, the thorned bamboo, shot straight up, and curved on top under the weight of the fanning leaves. Massive bushes huddled together beneath towering trees. There were elephant ears so large I could have disappeared behind a single one. Great ribbons of roots curved between the brush. Vines with sharp leaves curled around tree trunks or, leafless, hung down from great heights like rope, reaching down to attack a stump, a branch, an arm twisting upward with sprays of pink petals. Small plants and shoots came up everywhere; over every inch of earth there was a tangled screen of dead twigs, branches, leaves. The smell of decay mixed with the dampness. Rotting trees slanted through the jungle. Poles of lifeless cane criss-crossed over the trail. Yellow moss crept over bark; mushrooms clustered in cracks.

Walking was slow. Vines tripped me, the paca tore my clothes. I sank in mud up to my knees; I crawled under interlacing saplings and swordlike caña-brava. The undergrowth caught at my knapsack and held me. Streams cut through the bush; some were only ankle deep, others were up to my waist and were cold and swift. Trails ended at these streams, and I was frustrated trying to find them again in the confused tangle of foliage on the other side. I went downstream, upstream, back and forth, looking for a sliced stalk of cane that meant a human being had once passed through. I breathed heavily, thought Damn! Maybe that hotel owner was right after all, but I quickly pushed that aside, certain that I would find the trail again and thinking, always: Don't panic, don't panic.

There were spiderwebs everywhere, often like a veil of gauze hanging across the trail. They left irritating fibers on my face and hands. There were small hairy spiders with long hairy legs, black shiny scarabs that I was too exhausted to examine but vaguely remembered from Egyptian paintings, beetles mottled yellow and black, giant beetles the color of gold, hosts of insects so strange they seemed like miniatures of monsters come from Mars. Blue grasshoppers jumped at almost every step I took, sometimes showers of them.

While walking, I was too absorbed with the trail itself to look or listen. I watched where I put my feet, and I bent low or crawled to keep from being scratched and torn. Only when I sat to rest or eat a disc of bread, the only food I had with me besides the farina, did sounds and sights become distinct. Chattering, howling monkeys grouped in trees and scurried along branches. Macaws screeched angrily. Wild turkeys rested high above me. Iguanas and small lizards raced noisily over dried leaves. The monkeys followed when I moved. The trail ran uphill and down, slippery, treacherous. Moss-covered logs spanned rivulets as bridges.

Late that first afternoon I came upon a lean-to made by passing Indians. It was no more than a few leaves tied to branches, held at a slant by thin poles.

The patch of earth beneath was not comfortable. It was made as a shelter against the rain, and that night it rained heavily.

It is difficult for me now to remember my thoughts during that first night as I lay there, shivering slightly with cold. I wasn't happy and now I want to forget that time, to push it away as if it had never been. Of course, nothing happened; there were no snakes, no tigers, no headhunters, no tarantulas. Yet my mind overflowed with all these possibilities, and I must have lain awake for four or five hours before exhaustion forced me into sleep. During those sleepless hours, my eyes opened at every suggestion of movement that came my way. The rain stopped after a while, but drops of water, falling from the growth above, struck the leaves of the lean-to with force. Relax, I kept telling myself. Breathe deeply. Close your eyes and shut your ears. Breathe and sleep. It has been a long and tiring day, not the easy kind of day you'd expected. There is no need to push on. There is plenty of food. Relax. You'll get to the mission all right. No need to worry. Easy, take it easy. Don't walk so fast. Breathe in. Out.

When I got up in the morning, my shoulders ached, the muscles of my legs ached. Even my brain seemed to ache. My lips were cracked and my body was covered with scratches. I found a river, not my guide, and bathed and soothed myself in its waters. I sat and ate a chunk of farina and drank the water of the river. The sun was already high above the trees. In spite of my physical discomfort, I felt fine.

There followed eight days of a strange and inexpressible solitude. Not quite loneliness, which I'd understood throughout my life, but a feeling of apartness, a disconnection from life. I began to recognize and avoid the light-barked trees in which the soldier ants lived, and the tiny red ants that bit so fiercely. I still struggled with the paca, but I learned to back out of it rather than to go forward, so that the thorns left only needle-like holes in my shirt and trousers. I watched for the short, projecting stubs of branches that pulled at the straps of my knapsack. It no longer mattered that my feet, my clothing, got wet. Coming upon the first stream of a morning, or waking up beside one, and knowing that all day I would continue to wade through water and mud, I deliberately splattered myself and stood in mud-holes until, when I walked, the slush oozed out and caked on the canvas of my sneakers. It was a pleasant sound, that oozing.

It rained again and continued to rain through most of the following day. It was a warm rain, never heavy, and once I was soaked it was not even a source of annoyance. The rain and my wetness became a part of the landscape, and I accepted it as I accepted the herons, the parrots, the trees, the dawn, and my own walking through it all. I ate a piece of farina at daybreak and another in the evening. With water, it swelled up in my stomach so that hunger pangs were vague and timid signals indicating the need for food. My cigarettes got soaked and useless, a dozen packs of them. I saved the tobacco but felt no urgency to smoke. My sketching paper, a whole ream of it, got wet, and when dried took on a nice antique quality, brown at the edges.

There was an unreality to everything around me, and to myself as well. I felt like another person, not like myself at all, and though the world and my walking through it was always hazy and undefined, it never had the shape of a dream. It was as if I were off in another dimension, and I and the things around me were slightly out of focus. And mixed with these sensations was the curious feeling of being more alive, of a oneness with this sensuous and quivering world, of moving with it, rather than within it.

The trail was half through jungle, half along beach, almost always covered with stones. There would be two or three kilometers of pushing through the undergrowth, two or three of walking along the beach, and always the crossing of rivers. Once or twice armadillos peeked out from behind bushes, monkeys continued to follow, and toucans, in pairs, sat in trees crying out in raucous voices or scraping beak against beak.

I slept in a lean-to only that first night. After that, I stamped down a square of jungle and slept with the large elephant ears over me in case of rain. Or, clearing away stones, I slept on the warm sand of the beach. By the end of the second day my muscles were feeling more normal, and when I awoke on the third morning, all the pains were gone. Walking became pure joy.

Early one drizzling afternoon, I had just come from the darkness of the jungle into the openness and brilliance of a beach. A flock of parrots fluttered from the top of the forest, settled for a moment, then with great shrieks flew across the river and settled once again. White herons dotted the river, others floated down from the sky like sheets of paper caught by drafts of wind. Suddenly I saw a jaguar, some fifty feet away, at the water's edge. Its reflection glittered and arced out in ripples. A jaguar lapping with a long, quick tongue. As I stood and watched I slipped on stones, and at the grating noise of rock against rock the jaguar's head jerked up. He looked around, attached his eyes to the unfamiliar figure and stared at me. He turned slowly back down to the water and went on drinking, then stopped nervously after a few laps and looked up at me again. Frightened, fascinated, I barely breathed. Again the head came up to look at me. Slowly, the jaguar backed up, turned, and disappeared into the jungle.

On rare occasions I saw snakes slithering across the trail or wrapped lazily around the branches of a tree—boas, I thought to myself. I stopped once in front of a twig that wiggled on the ground. Startled, the snake lay there motionless a full two minutes, as I stood motionless above it, before it moved on under dead leaves. A week later, when Manolo and I were out walking together, we came upon another one just like it. A coral snake, he said.

There were few signs of human life: a dried footprint, only one in fact, enough to startle me; a sliced bit of branch or stalk; a small grove of banana trees that grew wild, obviously abandoned for many years. I spent the night in that grove, gorging myself on its fruit.

There were many rivers and streams to cross, most of them no higher than my waist. Sometimes, though, the current was so strong it pushed me downstream, and the mud was so like quicksand that a twenty-foot expanse of water would take fifteen minutes to cross. But I no longer thought about time or delay. There was no need to hurry on.

At times, when the sun was hot and my clothes wet only with perspiration, I stopped to wash out my shirt and underwear and bathe, more for pleasure than in need. I left the clothing in the water, held in place by rocks. I lay down in the cool shallow water, with the sun beating down, and watched the bird life sail and swoop across the blue or pink of the sky. I wanted to reach out, and did stretch out my arms to catch the birds, to rub their feathery bodies against my chest, my stomach. I picked up stones and threw them into the distance. I pushed logs into the river and watched them float down with the current. I imitated herons standing one-legged, and let myself fall backward, keeping the bird's posture, stiff, like a statue. I splashed along the water's edge and rolled over and over, back and forth, in and out of the sand, then jumped into deeper water. I skipped up and down the beach to dry myself, my arms stretched out, breathing deeply the warm, dizzying air, my flesh tingling under the intoxicating stimulation. I became a part of the voluptuous orgy, and I luxuriated in it.

The days seemed to have neither beginning nor end. They floated one into the other. Sleep was only a pause, its limits set by the seconds it took to fall into blankness, and the shrugs to clear my head as rays of light streaked through the trees. All my body needs were attended to. I could have gone on endlessly, roaming through that incredible forest I was coming to understand. One afternoon, when the sun had moved to about three o'clock, I sighted smoke. The cloud of blue rising from the green came as a shock. Even now, I'm not sure whether that shock was one of delight or disappointment.

I went through a patch of yuca bushes shaded by papaya and banana trees. Dogs barked, and I made out the top of the first hut. I had reached the mission.

This veranda on which I have been writing and thinking all afternoon is an open end of the second story of the building in which the white people of the mission live. Father Moiseis' room is just the other side of the partition, a wall of vertical slats of bark tied, with vines, to branches. Next to his is the room in which I sleep, followed by the rooms of Manolo and Hermano. The whole building is made of various parts of the palmera tree: walls and floors are strips of bark and the roof is a thatch made of its leaves. In my room a mattress of bark is set upon short logs, and I sleep between sheet and blanket. A wooden box, emptied of rifle shells, is my night table, and holds candle and book, an old chipped ashtray, a glass. A small tree, its branches cut short, leans into a corner. On it I hang my extra shirt and trousers. A hole cut into a wall looks down on the Rio Rojo.

On the floor next to my foot is a stack of religious magazines, and next to them is an ancient victrola. Records, also piled on the floor in uneven stacks, vary from Peruvian huaynos and marineras to Caruso and Toscanini conducting Bach—records pressed in 1911. The one other table holds Manolo's typewriter, and above it is a shelf of often-read books: Thomas à Kempis' *Imitation of Christ*, Camus' *The Plague* (both of these in French), editions of the Old and New Testaments in various languages, the Vulgate, *Steppenwolf* (in Spanish), Gide's *Journals* and *Corydon, The Life of St. Paul*, some pocket books of science fiction and detective stories (all in English), and a book of Greek plays in Greek.

Manolo has just come back into the clearing below me, waving his hand, asking if I want to go swimming. I yell back that I'll be down in a minute.

I can see from here that Patiachi has finished cutting up the tapir and there are women around him, bending to gather up the sections of bamboo. Three men sit next to a fire in front of the building we call the pharmacy and are gluing paujil feathers to the ends of shafts with black, raw wax. The sun has turned to a disc of red and now floats atop the forest. To the beach, before it gets too dark to bathe!

2

Now that I've begun this diary, these letters, whatever they are, it is difficult to know how to go on. There is so much that is stored unsorted within me, ready to burst and sprawl across these pages so that my pen attacks the paper as if of its own accord. And why continue on at all, when it might be better to seek my answer and to describe myself over a canvas that now waits for paint like a tethered boar set to entrap a leopard?

And I think of all those who will read this. My friends, that is. You, that is. Because when I have got as far with myself as I want to go, or as far as I can go, I intend to remove it, this part of my life, by sending the manuscript somehow up over the mountains, across the seas, to those who will understand it. And when I put the name Manolo down it is C who comes quickly to mind, and I want to rush headlong into telling of Manolo, forgetting everything else. Or thoughts of M will make the words pile up to tell of this fantastic landscape, to describe the indescribably various greens and yellows, and maybe I think: Oh, M! we must do this together, a book with all the nuances of living in so remote a region, so bright in its palette of images, so gay and gentle the simple day from mist-grey sunrise, through the pattern of food and work, on to the quick sucking of the sun by the forest. Or the thought of C will envelop me and out should pour the bits of anthropological data: the descriptions of the weirdly painted figures who sit with bodies interlaced, and sleep with loving arms and legs adjusted through other pairs of limbs and torsos, a human warp and woof, confused and cluttered by streams of hair, by bones and teeth and shells and seeds, all necklaces brightening the dark skins.

There will be no pretense of objectivity here. My memory is faulty, my mind continues as always to accept only the thoughts that pass through its narrow channel. Listen!

Out here in this lost and found world of chattering monkeys, shrieking birds, and Indians with undirected attitudes, its seems unlikely that I exist at all, that pen and paper are now at work, that a time might come when these papers will fit together and become a manuscript that will travel away beyond me, beyond my control of reader and interpretation. Yet it is true—Manolo, Father Moiseis, Hermano, are people only to me; their names I made from other names, and Piqul Mission is a place that I have set within the limits of this country of Peru.

It is not my intention to deny any past, for you, my friends, know of my grant to come and paint in Peru. A year has passed since my arrival in Lima, but it is no more than a month that I have been here at the mission. This is the second day of my writing; two days ago I decided that I would move on, but that I would remain somewhere within this jungle for the rest of my days. Laugh if you will. I know that at my age of thirty-five it is no simple matter to turn my life upside down, to put aside all the external aspects of my past. Yet everything here feels so right to me. If this were my first trip into such an area this sudden decision would certainly be suspect, and I would wait a longer time to make it, until some of this enchantment wore off. Here, life and the jungle have so exhilarated me with their wildness that I feel almost boundless energy and love; I feel capable of all manner of eccentricity, capable of living with and through any inconvenience, any difficulty, that might arise.

There has been no problem, as I had thought there might be, of time on my hands. I live without thoughts of earning my daily bread, with few books to read—and these mostly in Spanish, a language in which I am hardly fluent, but which is coming easier to me each day since it is the language we speak at the mission. The days pass slowly, evenly, and pile up quickly. I sketch, take long walks, talk a bit with the Indians and try to learn the language, laugh at childish Indian pranks, go off on short trips with Manolo, chop wood, make flutes out of paca stalks and practice playing old tunes. Most afternoons, during siesta, when even the noisy macaws are almost silent, I just lie on the hammock on the veranda and look down at the Rio Rojo cutting its vermilion path through the greens to where it swerves, opens out and meets the great and furious Hijo de Dios. There is a fullness to the days, a delight in everything around, that forces patience and ease. Manolo has been tireless in his talk and companionship. The world is beautiful and the sun shines gloriously. I love it all—the Indians, Manolo, the birds, the animals, the forest itself. My love bursts out in all directions; I even will some of it to fall upon Hermano and Padre Moiseis. Will I take it with me, this love, when I go off alone?

And now, with my whole being filled with the idea of leaving, it has become important for me to get this diary up to date as soon as possible. Since Wassen's arrival and his story of the slaughter of every person in his village while he was out collecting herbs, I feel that I should be spending all my time writing so that I can get it down, everything that's happened, before I begin my search for the Akaramas. It is becoming the realization of a dream, my being here, it's as if I were back in *Bomba the Jungle Boy*, my favorite reading in my early teens. To me the events of this time have been profound and intense, though I cannot sort them out or tell their meaning. My mind is not a logical one. It allows most things to pass through without sifting them into proper categories, without analysis. I must add to this diary in the same way that I slowly add to and organize a painting, build it up brush stroke by brush stroke to its final stage. Sometimes, after a sketch has been put onto a canvas, I work just in one corner for hours—days—at a time, then try another area, hoping to keep the original composition. Every time a new stroke goes down the whole effect changes and I get more excited, and the whole idea of the painting can turn into something I'd not had in mind when I began. For me it is the process of creation that is remarkable and exciting—infinitely more so than the final product. It is true enough that I do enjoy the finished work, and I am always a little astonished when I stand back and look, and tell myself it's done, and scribble my name in the lower right hand corner. I cannot intellectualize a canvas while at work upon it, nor can I after its completion. I have to feel my way along, expecting my instincts to show me the right direction. It may not be the way to put together a diary or manuscript, but I must tell my own story in this same way; perhaps you will connect it all together and analyze my motives and methods.

In my life in New York it had been a need of mine to appear sensitive and shy—the opposite of aggressive. My path had always been a narrow one, a trail I'd hacked out to avoid as much pain and suffering as possible. If I were ever to return to that world would I go back as well to those same old thinking habits? Is it possible for anyone ever to really change? I still have certain prejudices here, though they no longer come from reading Eliot, or *The Nation,* or from my feeling worldly, or from being a painter. My prejudices are different now and come from these new surroundings, from the macaw down in front of the pharmacy, from that huito tree on the other side of the Rojo, from Wassen looking up to show me a nutria he has just killed, from the color of that banana leaf that keeps changing from yellow to green to yellow to green—changing with only this slight wind to move it from sunlight to shade and back again into sun. I'm not much of a painter any longer. That pretentiousness of mine appears to be gone, though I do sketch each day. And when I go off alone I will take this paper not only to write on, but also as something on which I will draw.

How I wish it were possible at this moment to send off an ordinary letter to one of you and get an answer next week! M! you have always seen things so clearly. Tell me now why I am so desperate to leave this place! Tell me why even now I am bothered by my lack of understanding of Father Moiseis and Hermano! After all these weeks of living here I have no insight into either of them. Is it only senility and solitude that have given Father Moiseis this aura of madness? Has the jungle rot penetrated his skull and started, within, a process of decay? Are there little fungi growing all over his brain? Is Hermano nothing more than an extension of the father? Is he so horrified at the hunch on his back that he wants to disappear completely inside another's shadow? Are my thoughts now nothing more than continuing prejudice? But wait, I am going too far ahead. Wait, M, I will tell it all.

When I arrived at the mission, it was strange and disturbing to come upon people after so many days of absolute solitude, even though it had been my plan to come here, knowing there were at least a priest and a number of Indians. Of course I knew it. It was where I wanted to go, to come, but still it took me several days to relax. It was only with Manolo that I was able to think and listen and talk. It was he who gave form to the impressions that were coming at me so quickly, he through whom I was able to settle my mind and my body. To me he was less a part of the surroundings and more familiar in appearance and ideas. Father Moiseis, with his incessant flow of words, and Hermano, silent and furtive in manner, represented a vagueness, something undecipherable, a background against which I would live, a scene that commingled with the background of the jungle, the rest of the people, the animals.

Confused and disturbing as that first afternoon and evening here at the mission were, they come back to me now with amazing clarity. I was surrounded immediately by Indians and barking dogs, even before I reached the mission clearing itself. The men were dressed in torn khaki shirts and trousers. They had long hair, and some of them had designs painted in red or black on their faces. They just stood around me, with curious eyes and uncertain gestures, saying nothing, maybe waiting for me to say something or to go on to meet the man they knew I must have come to see. While I was standing there, full of curiosity myself, I heard shouts of "Ola!" and over the trail an old man in a white beard came running, his dirty cassock held above his knees.

"Ola! Ola!" He kept yelling, "What's this! Ola! What's this! Eh! Manolo! Manolo! Hermano! Come quick! Come! Ola!! Ola! What's this!" He ran right up and hugged me and bounced up and down, threw his arms around me again, looked at the Indians and laughed, and hit me several times on the shoulder.

"Ola! Oye! Caracho! Come! you must be hungry and tired, come sit down! What are you doing here? Where did you come from? Ola! Manolo! Hermano! Come quick, quick! Caracho!"

He put a sweat-drenched arm around me, squeezed me, held me off to look at me, hugged me again, pulled me toward the compound. A young, bearded man came from behind a hut, followed by a tiny hunchbacked older man.

"Mira! Mira!" the father yelled. "Look what I have found! He just grew up out of the jungle!"

Dogs snarled and barked. The Indians began to laugh. The face of the bearded young man beamed at me. "Well! how do you do! I'm Manolo. This is Hermano, the sacristan. Father Moiseis you already seem to know."

"But come, come, we must give the young man something to eat," said the padre, leading me by the hand into a small hut in the center of the compound. My first footsteps touched fishbones, then bones of animals of all sizes, wads of cotton, leaves, shells, mud, bits of paper, all scattered on the floor like a carpet. There were spiderwebs in all four corners. A window was held open with a piece of string. Outside all the

Indians gathered, male and female, some at the door, some at the window, pushing each other, hugging each other, giggling and shy.

There was an open shelf in the wall that divided the diningroom from the kitchen; there a bodiless hand held out enameled plates full of fried yuca, which Hermano took and placed upon the log table. Later, a pot of tea appeared upon the shelf.

"And so you have come into our jungle, eh?" The hair of Father Moiseis stuck out wildly, full of bits of twig and leaf. He wore small, steel-rimmed glasses; his beard came down to his chest. With a gnarled hand he would push the beard into his mouth and chew it as he talked. Pieces of yuca fell into the growth as he ate, and he used it to wipe the wetness of the tea from his lips. His head tilted first to one side, then to the other. The Spanish words came out endlessly, in an unpunctuated flow.

"Cha! but we have here so much to show you, the chacras are doing so well this year, even though my boys won't work, but how can you expect them to work when everything is so easy and all they have to do is pick some fruit and put a branch of yuca in the ground and up it grows in a few days, but Dios mio! I've been here for forty years, forty years in this jungle, and in Lima they said, No, no you must not, cannot go there, caray! We can't help you, no, there is no need for a mission there, the people are no good, they are dangerous—can you imagine my Indians being dangerous? No, no they are simple people, look at their faces, did you ever see such honest faces, and if sometimes they won't work it doesn't matter, there is no need, they pick the fruit, plant a branch. They said in Lima, Oh no, we cannot send you out there, and here I am now in this mission ten years with Manolo and Hermano but here all time is the same, and days and weeks and years are nothing and in Lima they said, No no—aren't they like little dolls, these savages of mine, they say they are savages but maybe some day here or there you will see real savages, there are some not so far away!"

There was neither period nor pause in his talk. His voice was musical and ran up and down the scale. He shook his head and hands and chewed his beard. The repetitions permitted me to distract myself with glances at the others. Manolo looked about thirty-five. He wore a blue shirt open to the rope that held up his pants. There were no buttons on the shirt; maybe one on his pants. His sneakers were full of holes and some toes stuck out. He had a short black beard, trimmed in Vandyke fashion. Very curly hair, in need of cutting at the neck and around his ears, sat on his head like a helmet. Hermano stood an inch or two under five feet. He had a large head that was set onto his shoulders without a visible neck. His patched shirt was split down the back as if by the strain of his hump. Small eyes darted back and forth, and he laughed at everything the padre said.

"Mas té, padre?" The head of an old woman appeared over the shelf of the opening into the kitchen. Her long hair covered most of her face.

"Si, si, more tea, more tea, Santusa. Santusa used to

work for Señor Palomino, was a slave of Señor Palomino, was chained up at night with the others but she got away one night when they were using her and forgot the chain afterwards—but that was more than a year ago—Señor Palomino chased her with dogs and rifles, but she escaped—a smart one—and then she came here, ai caracho! But she can tell you some stories from all her years there and of all the babies she had, but you are tired no? and you will rest before we have our supper?"

Father Moiseis went on to the storage room to see if there were any ripe papayas for supper. Manolo sat next to me on a log.

"You probably want to lie down for a while."

"Just sitting here is all the rest I need now. Tell me about the padre. Does he speak all these Indian languages?"

"Oh, just a little. I'd say most of the time he makes himself misunderstood. But he is a remarkable man, for having spent so many years in the jungle. He hates the outside world, and the few times a year he has to go to Cuzco or Lima he's miserable, and comes back without having done any of the things he went to do in the first place. He does love the people here but he can't see them as they are, only as he hopes they are. Of course he has no control over them at all. They have a pretty easy life here, it's the only reason they stay, and all of them feel superior to the other Indians in the jungle since they have machetes, and pots and pans, and wear clothes most of the time. Maybe years ago he was a good missionary, according to what the Church thinks of as a good missionary, but here he just lives on, using up his time until he dies, I guess. Which is probably what I'm doing myself."

"Well, what *are* you doing here?"

"Me? I'm a wanderer."

"Staying in one place for ten years doesn't sound like wandering to me."

"Of course, you're right. Ask me another time."

Hermano stood on the veranda above us, looking down. When I turned to stare at him he moved away, and disappeared into one of the rooms.

"Hermano has been with the padre for all of the padre's forty years in South America. He comes from a mining town in the mountains above Lake Titicaca. Both of his parents were killed in some kind of explosion there, when he was about five. Father Moiseis happened to be visiting a mission not far away and this was his first disaster. Apparently Hermano attached himself to him, and they've been together ever since. Never apart, even after all these years, except when the padre goes to Lima. He's never known anything but mission life, never been anywhere on his own. Now he's even more devout than the padre, who's become too lax to think of what day of the week it is or to worry about things like fish on Friday. I feel sorry for him, but that's the only feeling for him I have. He works hard all day long. He thinks that by watching the Indians he can stop them from doing anything he calls sin, which assumption is a big joke, as you'll see soon enough.

"But why don't we go up while it's still light and

I'll show you where you will sleep. By now you know there aren't any conveniences around, and I hope you won't be bothered by it. We wash in the river and use the bushes downstream for our toilet."

After depositing my knapsack on the floor of my room, he showed me his own room, separated from mine by a thin partition of bark, the kind of wall that separated all the rooms. The partitions were covered with bows, arrows, gourds, and red and black carrying bags woven of fiber. There was a bark bed with mosquito netting above it, and a real chair piled with books—some in French, some in Spanish, some in English.

"So you speak English, Manolo?"

"No, no. I can understand enough for reading, but that's all. Maybe I can learn a little while you're here."

I looked closely at a small portrait in oil.

"A self-portrait, done seventeen or eighteen years ago. I used to paint. Sometimes now I write stories. Nothing to do with the life here. Surrealist stories. In French, in case the padre happens upon them. Maybe some day you'd like to read one or two. I'm afraid he wouldn't approve of some of my books either, but none of the strange ones are in Spanish."

Someone below rang a tinny bell.

"That's supper. Let's go."

3

The next morning Father Moiseis did not budge from the diningroom after breakfast. He sat and talked, and his soliloquy went rushing on until it was almost time for lunch.

"Caracho! But it is peculiar to have a stranger here; there hasn't been anyone since Father Francisco over a year ago. Forty years I've been here in jungles of Peru, I was twenty-nine when I came to South America from Spain, it was a long time ago. And not so many years ago—1940? 1943? I don't remember, Hermano could tell you maybe, there was that expedition that came with all those scientists from your country and from Europe and from Canada—they said Canada is such a beautiful country, like the Sierra here with much snow—he was a nice man that Canadian, he'd spent some time in Spain. Ah when I think of Spain, of my home and my mother always in black, weeping, crying for food, but no, here is my home, and Spain is such a good country. The scientists went to the government in Lima and the government told them I was the only one who could lead them into the jungle and show them the savages—I remember when

I was a boy in Seville and we used to play in the streets and my mother would shout from the window —so the government gave them twenty soldiers, twenty soldiers! What did they need protection for with me with them? And they all flew with their big equipment to Cuzco and then there was no road after Paucartambo, and they had to walk down and down the mountains to Pasñiquti and their feet hurt so much and had such sores on them, they did not have much experience, even the soldiers had difficulty walking, not like me after so many years. I had my mission in Pasñiquti then, where there was no civilization like now with the haciendas all around—and a place to get drunk and go whoring, ugh! But then we moved to Madrid, a beautiful city, when I was ten years old— that Canadian he was such a good man, we talked for days about Madrid, and all the museums, and El Greco. I told them all that we would go to visit the Mashcos, whom no one had ever seen before, only me, and only I knew how to speak their language, and they are savages even now and don't trust anyone but me—you should see one time, señor, it would make such a pretty picture for you: a woman with a baby at one breast, a little monkey at the other, don't you like that for a picture? You will paint it? This tea is good, no? I brought it with me last year all the way from Lima—the time Father Francisco came. And so I told the scientists that if I was going to take them farther into the jungle to the Mashcos they would have to let me talk first with them for a while, maybe a whole day, to prepare them for so many visitors and soldiers—they don't trust anyone, you see, fighting and killing all the time, that's all they know, no God, my poor little ones, they know nothing of God and our dear Lord Christ. Did you like our yuca last night, just like fried potatoes, no? Another picture you will paint is that of another woman, with a baby at one breast and a snake at the other, no? A beautiful picture, caray! They are afraid snakes will take the mother's milk in the night when she's asleep, so when the mother is nursing a baby they put some of her milk in the doorway; the snakes drink that at night and don't bother the mother, a pretty picture, no? So, caracho! We had to take so many rafts for all those soldiers, what did they need so many soldiers for when their protection was me, and such equipment they had with them! Generators and recording machines to take their voices, they said, you have heard of them? They tried them out at the mission in Pasñiquti and all my people, not savages but my people, who loved God, were frightened—I don't know what else they had but so much, so much! They were going to make records of the way my people talked, and all the time the soldiers had their guns out shooting at the herons and the parrots, what for? I asked them and they said they were practicing, you know, with their guns. We had to hunt so much food for so many people—not with their guns, because they were never able to kill anything, but with the bows and arrows of my Puerangas. Ten days later—ten days it took—we saw the Mashcos there on a beach. But that was a long time ago, so many years ago, before there was any Señor Palomino, before there was any civilization here at all you understand. Well do you think that my friend the Canadian and the others waited for me as I had told them to wait? Oh no, they went ahead on their rafts, in such a hurry, oh yes, they had to be the first, and I warned them, I told them I should be the first, but no, they raced on, telling my Puerangas to pole faster and faster and caracho! Those savages—I told them—saw the rafts, and so many men, and they shot off their arrows; and then the soldiers, you know with their guns, they couldn't wait—I told them—they shot their guns and the rafts—*Dios mio*! The rafts turned over, all but mine they turned over, and lost that equipment costing so much money— but I told them. Wouldn't that make a beautiful picture that baby at one breast and a snake at the other? You will paint it? And ya! The Mashcos disappeared after that and went further into the jungle, and now when they look up into the sky and see an airplane they say apak-tone, old father, I am their old father, and I knew it, it was a fiasco, that great expedition with all that equipment and so many men, and they had to go back with almost nothing, only with the bows and arrows I gave them—but I told them, I did."

Somewhere in the middle of this rush of words Hermano and Manolo had come into the dining-room and were waiting patiently for another pot of tea to appear. Hermano had been laughing as he remembered the expedition, and a glow of satisfaction at its failure seemed to surround him. Manolo simply looked bored, as if he had heard these tales many times before.

A small boy in a pair of shredded shorts, with red spots painted on his face, came to the door and stood there shyly, leaning against the jamb. He held a hand up to his open mouth and glanced at me whenever he felt I was looking elsewhere. The padre poured fresh tea into his cup and offered it to the boy. He came over, took two quick sips, and ran out of the room.

"Oh, caracho!" the padre went on, "But there was never such equipment in all the world and you should have seen their faces when those Mashcos began shooting their arrows, all of them at once, and they took up their guns, they were so frightened, but what is there to be frightened of, my little people are no savages, they too were frightened, and why not with all those guns and men? I showed them a crucifix once and I told them it is God that little figure, they can understand the tiny figure being God—a God can be any size or shape. Whenever they see a plane—maybe one time in a year a plane goes by here—they think it is a big crucifix and I am there floating with it up in the sky."

Abruptly, as if he had just remembered something urgently to be done, the padre got up and went outside. Hermano followed. Manolo and I sat for a while, finishing our tea, with half-smiles on our faces, not talking, until a tiny woman with a baby straddled across her hip came to the door. A series of criss-cross lines was painted on her face, and she seemed as if she were waiting for someone to come and play tic-tac-toe upon it. Her long-sleeved mother hubbard had two holes torn or cut out at the breast, which revealed her large nipples and allowed her to suckle her baby without undoing the dress. Bones and shells decorated her shoulders.

"Paudisme, Da Mano," she whispered.

"Believe it or not," Manolo said to me, "that's Spanish she's speaking. 'Paludismo, Don Manolo,' is what she said." He got up, poured some tea into a fresh cup, and motioned her toward the pharmacy outside. A huge padlock held the door closed. Manolo took out a key and opened it. The inside was swept clean. There was one shelf of jars of drugs and a couple of tin boxes. The woman sat on a bench and watched Manolo open a small bottle of metoquine pills.

"These malaria pills are damned good. Much better than quinine ever was."

The baby was naked except for several strands of tooth and seed necklaces, and bands of lizard skin, which almost everyone wore as protection against snakes, around its wrists. Manolo took two of the pills and gave them to the mother, along with the cup of tea. She bent her head way back and dropped both pills into her open mouth. Then she took a drink of tea and bent her head back again to swallow.

"Wawa, Da Mano," she said, holding up the baby.

He gave her another pill, which she stuck down the throat of the baby, who coughed it up and began to scream. She tried again and up it came again. Then

Manolo tried, and the baby screamed even louder. "Damn!" he said under his breath. Together they inserted the pill and held the baby's mouth closed but it struggled so that they finally gave up. Manolo threw what was left of the pill out the door and took a small metal box from the shelf. He opened it and showed the needle and syringe to the frightened woman. She hugged the baby to her chest and rubbed its left shoulder. Manolo lit a candle and sterilized the needle. He poured alcohol through the glass tube and dabbed the thin arm with wetted cotton. He pinched a piece of flesh between his fingers and quickly, expertly, jabbed the needle into it. He withdrew the needle, placed it with its syringe back in the box, and the mother left the room, moaning as if it had been her pain, rubbing her own left shoulder.

After lunch the mission was silent in siesta. It was hot when I woke up. Not a leaf stirred. I took my towel and soap and happily went down to the river for my first bath. Two women were at the edge beating clothes on rocks. Some men were in the water, wearing black shorts much too large for them, fishing with three-pronged ebony spears. I took off all my clothes and went in to wash. Hermano appeared from behind a clump of papaya trees and squatted down to stare at me. The women got up and went farther downstream, around a bend, where I could no longer see them. The men waded up the river, far out of sight. Hermano continued to watch me and for an instant, from the distance, I thought I saw a tear fall down his cheek.

"Señor," Father Moiseis said to me later, "we do not show ourselves here to anyone, either men or women, not even here inside the hut. It is a sin, and you must be very careful!"

Lying in bed that night, reading by candlelight Manolo's Spanish edition of *Steppenwolf,* I heard laughter, splashing and running noises from the beach below. I got up and looked out my window. The night was clear, and a crescent moon hung low in the sky. Men and women, naked, were swimming, sitting in the sand, lying in the shallow water.

4

At dawn this morning I was, as usual, awakened by movement around me in other rooms—footsteps over the creaking floor and down the ladder, coughing and clearing of throats. I got up and put on my trousers, threw a shirt and towel over a shoulder, picked up soap, toothpaste and toothbrush and went down to the river. Father Moiseis, the long sleeves of his dirty white cassock rolled above his elbows, was kneeling on stones, washing his face without soap, cleaning his teeth with a finger. Hermano sat back from the beach on his haunches, half-hidden by bushes, as if he were emptying his bowels. Manolo was standing in the water, slightly stooped, cleaning his teeth with a yellow-handled brush. Two towels were spread on the sand. No one turned to look at or greet me as I dropped my articles, and walked into water up to my ankles, and knelt to wash.

There were silhouettes of Indians splashing in the water downstream. The sky to the east glowed red except where thin streaks of purple ran along the horizon. Overhead, red and blue melted together, while around us clouds of pink mist rolled through treetops, grey and blue. Colors shifted slowly until the yellow ball of sun reached above the horizon and suddenly the light moved quickly, touching up grey shadows with deep blue, spreading green and yellow over all the foliage, changing the red sky into a transparent cobalt.

Hermano came out of the bushes to splash water on his face. He rubbed his hands dry and followed Father Moiseis toward the chapel. Manolo closed the only button on his pants, came over, smiling, and threw a handful of water at my head.

"I just remembered a good place for a swim today. Not very far. You can take sketching materials along if you like."

"Fine," I said, and bent to pick up my toiletries as the chapel bell began to ring. We hurried up the embankment to the small thatch building where the service had already begun.

The chapel was empty of all furniture or decoration except what was needed for the Mass itself. There were no pews, no candles, no stations of the cross. Father Moiseis mumbled in Latin while Hermano tended his needs upon the altar, a platform a slight step above the floor on which only Manolo and I stood and knelt. Outside a dog barked.

We breakfasted on fried bananas and bitter coffee, then Manolo and I went through a short piece of jungle, behind the mission, to a small beach at the sharp bend of the Rio Rojo, where three rafts were on the beach, tied with vines to large rocks. Each raft was about twenty feet long and less than three feet wide, and was made of four balsa logs tied together with vines, cross-pieced and pegged at each end. I slipped a vine off one of the rocks and we pushed a raft easily into the water.

The water rushed against the far red bank that forced the turn, churning violently over jutting rocks, dissolving the red clay that gave the water its curious color. On the other side, just before this turn, there was a gap in the jungle through which flowed another small river that emptied into the Rio Rojo. Manolo poled the raft across the Rojo, into the smaller river. At the turn I looked back and saw Hermano crouching on one of the beached rafts, staring at us.

The jungle leaped out all around us on all sides and arched over our heads. Parrots, toucans, herons, wild turkeys, sailed through the sky or sat high on branches. The current was not strong, and Manolo eased his push on the bamboo pole, lifting it out of the water and dipping it back in again with a startling gentleness, almost caressing it with his neck and breast.

We glided upriver, slowly, sensuously.

I stood near the front end, poling on one side of the raft and then the other, while Manolo maneuvered from the rear. The river was so narrow, and the jungle so close, we often had to bend to avoid branches. Only occasional patches of sky showed through above our heads. We continued along this curving waterway for almost an hour, watching the birds circle around us, at times seeing the eyes of a crocodile just on the water's surface, hearing the sounds that drifted from the forest. We came to a bank of mud and beached the raft, tied it to a tree. We climbed a small hill, thick with growth, then found a stream bed, hardly more than a trickle, that led to a great open area and a large pool.

The pool's center was a flat white stone, drawing down to it and reflecting rays of sunlight like an altar, brilliant under hidden lights. The water at the edge of the pool was in shadow, silken in texture. Blues faded gradually into the greens of the shadows from the surrounding jungle. Vines dropped from enormous trees straight down into the water. There was no beach—only large, smoothly rounded rocks that formed the wall that kept the growth from creeping further into the pool. At the edges bunches of leaves, dead or still green, crowded between the rocks and bobbed up and down with the slow rhythm of the water's movement. There were no sounds. Nothing stirred. Even the stream that flowed into it did so hesitantly, slowing often to move around a rock or crook, to slip over small stones and fallen branches.

We stood still a second, a minute, then removed our clothing and entered the pool without a word. The bottom deepened quickly and, after the first stunning shock of cold water, we pushed off and made for the rock in the center.

It came just then, a memory out of the past. Remember, C, that river in Mexico? Remember the trip we took to collect those orchids not far from Manzanillo? The orchids were so difficult to get at, and we were so hot and tired from climbing trees, and we came upon the river with the tree trunk across it all slippery with moss, and I fell off, ten feet down, and thought for sure I would drown, and I held those damned bulbs above my head, more afraid of losing them than of losing my life? Here the shock of cold water was my madeleine. And remember later you and I rested there, C, and we put our clothes on branches to dry in the sun, and went again into the water. My mind was no longer on what had happened, but only full of the excitement of the isolation, the wildness, the beauty on every side. And I thought then as we lay there side by side—my first time in any jungle—that there must be other, deeper forests for me, more isolated, more interior, where man was barely known. There we'd gone by jeep, yet how remote we thought it! I felt like that this morning. Sometimes, in my dreams of paradise, I used to see this very place—with palm trees reaching up so high and bending slightly, with giant mahogany and ebony covered with large-leafed vines, with ferns and canes and birds of paradise.

I am not a good swimmer. In the pool I headed straight for the great rock, was tired by the time I reached it, and pulled myself out of the water. Manolo swam and turned around in the water, a porpoise gaily returning to waters known from long ago. I lay down on the rock and blinked up at the sun. I stood, and stretched, and shouted at the top of my lungs to all the hidden animals, to all the world: "Here I am! Here I am! It's me!!"

Manolo came up laughing and pulled my arm and

down I splashed. The water was clear and we swam around each other just beneath its surface. He caught my ankle and dragged me down to where tiny yellow fish and larger speckled ones nudged our bodies, unsure of what these large, moving creatures could be. We climbed onto the stone and sat, dripping, sparkling. We sunned, went back into the water, sunned again, and slept. At noon we were back at the raft, silently making our way back to the mission. It was a rare morning.

It wasn't the first time Manolo and I had gone off alone together. Every day we walked, or took the canoe or raft, and spent hours away from the mission. But there was something different in me this morning, coming upon that pool as we did, so hidden away where Manolo's eyes were surely the only ones to have seen it. I had not discovered it myself but I became a part of it, savored its color, its heat and cold, our being in a place where no other humans could see us. But rare and beautiful as it was, some perverse streak within me longed for other days, times when I was completely alone, when not even a Manolo or a C was there to respond.

Remember when I walked across the Yucatan peninsula? Remember my delighted descriptions of my aloneness? And the paintings that evolved? If my experiences here are similar I know now that they are not really the same, that in Mexico too much of my time and energy were taken up with looking at things, with trying to record them for future paintings, for conversation, for something that had nothing to do with living in the present. I should have simply existed there in that world, absorbing whatever was around me. In Mexico it was all new to me; wherever I was there was never any thought in my mind but that people were close by. I knew that if I continued walking on for three or four hours I would come to a village, a hut, a plantation, some kind of outpost. It was different here, coming to the mission, walking day after day with barely a sign that people other than myself were anywhere on earth. This was my joy.

It is beginning to get dark. Only a few minutes of light remain. Last night after supper Manolo and I sat on the log bench below the veranda; the fireflies were out in full force and Chako ran around catching them and putting them into a glass jar—about twenty of them finally—which gave us almost enough light to read by. Women stood close to us, chewing grasshoppers and beetles. Patiachi's wife Itaqui, a delicate young girl about sixteen looking somewhat top-heavy with a great mass of hair covering most of her face, offered us a pair of beetles. I took one and squashed it between my fingers and plopped it into my mouth.

Manolo has been collecting ethnological material from the mountain and jungle people for years. In the evening he tells stories, and sings. Then others come from their huts to listen. Later they sing, sometimes dance. Last night he insisted for the first time that I join, and I started off with "Swing Low, Sweet Chariot." Then nothing else would come to me, until

I thought of Hebrew chants and went mournfully into "Vei ani s'feelosee-ee:"

And as for me, may my prayer unto thee, O Lord,
Be in an acceptable time:
O God, in the abundance of thy loving kindness,
Answer me in the truth of thy salvation.

It was a great success. Laughter and beating of sticks one against the other were the demonstrations of approval. Then Manolo started on a haunting, minor-key song he had learned when he had lived in the mountains near Cuzco:

> *Ripunay q'asa-patapi*
> *Saywaschallay rumi*
> *'Amama willankichu*
> *Mama taytaymanqa*
> *'Aswansi willaykunki*
> *Warma munasqayman:*
> *'Qonqa-qorachata*
> *Maskhay kuskan, nispa.*

> In the path of my departure
> Stands a boundary stone.
> But you will say nothing
> To my mother or my father;
> Rather, you will say
> To my beloved:
> "He is searching
> For an herb of forgetfulness."

I quickly learned to play it on a cane flute.

5

It comes closer now, the time of my departure.

Six days ago Wassen walked into the mission compound while we were still in the middle of our breakfast banana cereal. He was a thin old man with hair that dropped down to his chest and covered his forehead, reaching to his eyelashes. There were six long red and yellow feathers sprouting from around his mouth. He wore necklaces of red and black seeds, teeth of animals, monkey bones, snail shells, and bits of jaguar fur. The bones of his chest stood out, and his legs, except for the knobs of knees, were like stalks, which ended in feet with toes that spread like roots. His penis was tied up against his abdomen with a piece of fiber-like string that circled his foreskin and went around his waist. It was discolored from tattooing. The bag of his testicles hung like an almost empty sack of marbles, leaning flatly against his thighs. He slapped a hand to his chest and coughed several times. He laughed and wiggled his head back and forth, stroked his chest and put his other hand to his forehead and squinted as if in pain.

I think he was a surprise to us all. "Caracho! but

I've never seen one like him before! So many years I've been here and no one like this!"

Manolo got up and patted Wassen on the shoulder and said, "Iakiak, iakiak. Come." We all followed in fascination to the pharmacy. Others also came, all who were there at the compound, to look at him, the men all carrying their machetes or their bows and arrows.

Wassen was seated at the table and again he shook his head and the feathers on his face fluttered. Manolo got out his syringe and filled it with penicillin. He sat down next to Wassen and touched the feathers. Wassen took one out and a piece of bone remained in the flesh, the skin having grown almost completely around it. He put the feather back in and picked up the syringe and tested the point with a finger. Manolo called me over. He sterilized the needle, told me to drop my trousers, and plunged it into my buttock without injecting any of the liquid, demonstrating the harmlessness of the instrument. Again he sterilized the needle and made Wassen stand. Wassen remained rigid for some time, until after the syringe had been put back into its box. Then he blew air from his mouth and farted loud and long. He took out two of his feathers and covered Manolo's eyes with them for a second, then replaced them.

Father Moiseis then came up, placed his hands upon Wassen's shoulders, and kissed him on the mouth. Wassen pulled back and licked his lips. There had been no expression on his face since first he laughed, nor had there as yet been a single word.

Hermano was standing at the door with a pair of khaki trousers in his hands. He gave them to the padre, who held them out to Wassen; he looked at but did not touch them. Wassen undid the fiber that tied up his penis and offered it to Father Moiseis. He lifted the padre's cassock, but there were a pair of shorts beneath it. There was a strange silence in the gesture, in the room. Manolo looked as if he were about to burst into tears. Hermano was horrified.

Having lowered my pants some minutes earlier, it seemed quite natural that I should do so again. I stepped out of them and took off my shirt. The padre let out a grunt. Hermano let out a grunt. They left the room. Manolo smiled. Wassen came over and took my penis in his hand. He frowned, obviously wondering about the lack of foreskin. He examined it closely and wrapped the fiber around its head and then around my waist, pulling my penis flat up against my belly. I put my clothes back on and Wassen picked up the trousers that had been left by the padre. He held them under his arm and went outside.

The Indians had been cleared away by the padre and Hermano, and the compound was completely empty. Wassen walked slowly down to the bank of the river and placed his hands flat upon the water, slapped the palms together and rubbed them dry on his thighs. He came back to us and squatted in the shade and indicated that we also were to sit. My penis had begin to ache and it was awkward to squat. There was pain in my anus. Manolo could see my discomfort and smiled. "Relax. You can untie it later."

Wassen brushed away a clear space in the dirt, took out all six feathers and lined them up on the ground, arranging them so that they all curved in the same direction. He rubbed his penis until it enlarged slightly, pushed his testicles under himself and set his penis down so that its head rested on the earth. He picked up all of the feathers and juggled them, letting them fall at will, picked them up again and put them back around his mouth. He looked at us, first at one, then at the other, and began to talk. Wassen spoke slowly in a whispering voice, a language that Manolo understood, and he was able to translate between the pauses that were the only show of emotion in this lonely old man.

"Far away, far from here, far from where this place is, is my place, is where I sleep and where I eat, is where my women are, my brothers, my fathers, my children. It is one sleeping, and one sleeping more from here. Far away. It is not there today. Fire came and left nothing. Akaramas came and left nothing. It is not there today. When the sun comes up, I fill my stomach, and I go alone into the forest and find my medicines. These are my medicines that help with sickness, and with women, and when I am tired and cannot make my penis grow large and my sack is empty, and my medicines to help keep strange gods from my people, my medicines to tell of when the giant jaguar approaches or the vipers are near. My medicines told me of the Akaramas and I went quickly, running, but already the sun had moved, had moved way away, and there was fire and smoke when I came back to my place.

"My place is far from here. It is not my place now. The Akaramas had taken some of my women. Some of my women were there on the ground with holes in their bellies. My fathers were without heads. My children were broken. My brothers were gone and they are now inside the bellies of the Akaramas. I am here with all my body and my medicines have no more use."

Manolo got up and took Wassen by the arm and led him to a hut in which he could sleep. He lay down and closed his eyes.

"He'll get sick and die here," Manolo said. "He's the oldest Indian I've ever seen and he may be as old as the padre. You can see that he already misses his village and his people. He'll probably sit here by himself all the time. He'll have no one to talk to or to laugh with, and he can't go out hunting any longer. Besides, the people here will always be frightened of him. So he'll tell himself it is time to die, and he will."

Later, when Wassen was moving again around the compound, I told Manolo to ask him about the Akaramas.

"I do not understand," said Wassen. "Who are the Akaramas? We are a people. They are a people. We live in a place. They live in a place."

"Where?"

"Far from here."

"How far?"

"Three sleepings, maybe another sleeping. Their place is Hitapo, by the river. They live there and they do not go out except to hunt and kill. We always fear them. We do not know when they come. The other people also fear them. The moons pass and they go out to take women."

"Tell me again where they are."

Wassen picked up a twig and sketched a rough map of rivers in the dirt in front of him. He dug four small holes and, pointing at each in turn, said, "Sleep. Sleep. Sleep. Sleep."

Then and there my heart skipped several beats and I was scared to death. They are a people; they live in a place. How simple can it be? They are in a place only four sleepings away, and I would like to see them. All I have to do is go. Simple enough!

I didn't think much about it, that decision. I think the decision was made the moment I laid eyes on Wassen, when I knew that out there in the forest were other peoples more primitive, other jungles wilder, other worlds that existed that needed my eyes to look at them. A flash of real terror came over me. I flushed and shook for a few seconds. Neither Wassen nor Manolo seemed to notice. My first thought was: I'm going; the second thought: I'll stay there. No coming back ever. Death or life, it's all the same.

6

Dear C, let me tell you about Manolo: the big shock was that he looks so much like you. Same square jaw, and eyebrows running together over the bridge of the nose. About five ten or eleven, with broad shoulders and excellent figure, not too muscular. Eyes that seem, quickly, to probe beneath the surface. And of course, he is a lay missionary here now, just as you were for those two years in Yucatan where I'd sent you after my days with Father Salk. Remember I had tried to get that *Catholic Worker* lady to pay for your trip down but even with Father Salk's letter to her, she rejected the idea without even having seen you. But you got there, the same way that Manolo got here.

Every evening before dinner, unless I am writing here, Manolo and I have walked along the beach, back and forth, for the short stretch of a hundred and fifty feet or however long it is. Beyond this patch of clean sand, the jungle crawls down to the water's edge. We watch the sunsets on clear days, which are usually over by six-thirty, when the sun drops behind the distant trees. Often the Indians stand for a few minutes or sit for a longer time, on the upper level, just a few

51

feet above us, watching us go down the beach, then back, retracing our steps time and again. At first, they pointed at us and laughed, wondering what on earth we were doing, why we were walking when it was so much simpler to sit. Sometimes now, one of the men follows us, back and forth, back and forth. We talk.

Another time, I asked him, "What are you doing here?"

"Like I said, I'm a wanderer."

"Try again."

"What do you expect me to say? That it's such a nice easy life here? That I'm too lazy or weak to move on? That *is* the truth of it! I sit around on my ass, give out a couple of pills, take someone's temperature, give him an injection. I listen to that crazy old man talk on and on. And I have that little creep keeping his eyes on me all day long, afraid I'll screw with someone. How do I know what I'm doing here? I just can't move."

There was a long silence. A bell clinked, calling us to supper. "Saved again," said Manolo.

As we were leaving the chapel later, the beating of a drum began on the far side of the mission. Another drum, then another began. The beat was slow. The padre looked disgusted. "Masato! Caracho! It is beautiful, here in this moonlight, no señor?" The moon was almost full, lighting up the compound like a street lamp.

"Yes, it is beautiful. What are they playing their drums for? Is there some kind of ceremony tonight?"

"I don't know. I am not interested when they act so much like savages and drink their masato. Pagans!

I will go to my room now. Good night, señor, good night Manolo, good night Hermano!"

"Can we go see what they're up to?" I asked Manolo.

"Of course."

Behind one of the Pueranga huts was a cleared area where men with small drums under their arms were moving around in a circle. On one side a woman stood with a large gourd from which she poured masato into gourd cups. When a man completed a circle, he stopped to drink, then he re-entered the circle. The fires lit up the interiors of two low huts where the women were, but there were no sounds from within.

We sat on the ground, Hermano hovering behind us. A woman in a fiber cuzma, a garment that hung around her like a toga, offered us gourds and filled them. As she bent down, clusters of thin, yellowed bones rattled. Hermano remained aloof and shook his head. Soon he left.

"What is it?"

"Yuca juice. Taste it first, then I'll tell you how it's made."

It was acrid, a little like vinegar with some sugar in it, slightly yellow in color.

"Not bad."

"The women masticate the yuca and spit the juice into a vat. Then they let it ferment a while."

Pueranga men shave the hair above their foreheads, around the ears and neck, leaving a circular patch, almost the opposite of a tonsure. Then a band of paujil feathers is tied below the remaining hair. These short black feathers, very shiny, cover their foreheads like bangs, coming down to their eyelashes. Tonight, they were wearing only loincloths made of bark, instead of the usual shirts and shorts that hung so badly on their bodies. The only woman to be seen was the one serving the masato. When her gourd was empty, she crouched in front of one of the huts and it was refilled.

The seven dancers each held a drum under his left arm, beating the stretched monkey skin with the fingers of his right hand. Each man danced by himself, though he kept to the circle. He would trot a few steps, turn completely around, trot some more, turn again. After a while, one of the men would leave the circle and go into the hut. Another would shortly appear to replace him.

"What's going on, Manolo?"

"Sex."

"As simple as that? Doesn't the padre know what's going on? or at least our friend Hermano?"

"It's not very good propaganda for the mission, so he refuses to let his brain acknowledge it. This kind of dancing goes on any time they have enough yuca stored up for a good batch of masato. They'll go on dancing all night long and then they'll lie in the river all day tomorrow, sobering up and resting."

An hour passed, maybe more, during which we said nothing. We had each had a good many gourds to drink. Manolo put a hand on my knee.

"There isn't much to tell you of my life. I was fifteen when the communists came to our little village in Spain and killed off the whole of my family—my mother,

my father, three brothers, a sister, uncles, aunts.
Me too, they thought. They said my father was a spy,
and only because he happened to be cutting wood in
the forest one day and found their camp. After we
were all shot right in our homes, no one would have
anything to do with me, and so I had to bury them all
by myself, with a bullet still in my thigh. Then in
some kind of revenge I went and joined Franco's army
and there they thought I was smart enough to be
trained as a pilot. But nothing seemed right to me
there in Spain and there was no sense in anything, so
I took off one day and went to France and joined
their army and fought against the Germans until the
end of the war.

"A wanderer, I call myself. Well, I wandered then,
all over Europe, wherever there wasn't too much
trouble over my papers. One day, I just walked into a
monastery and trained to be a monk for three years.
That was back in Spain, and three years later they sent
me to the Sahara as a missionary. And that's where I
really began to wander. From one bed to another. Oc-
cupied beds, that is. I think it wouldn't have been so
bad for my superiors if my companions had been
females. So, back to Spain I went; or rather, was sent.
Then, I went to Chile to work in a factory. After that,
Peru on a whaling ship. In Cabo Blanco I taught skin-
diving to rich tourists until I heard about Father
Moiseis living out here in the middle of nothing but
jungle and more jungle, great spaces of nothing but
jungle and primitive people.

"You know, it really hasn't been so difficult, all these

years. Every once in a while, I do get an urge for civilization, and I sit down and try to write a story. You know, all in symbolic terms, about the desert sand washing me clean after every little affair with an Arab boy. Of course you must have realized by now that I'm not so pure here either, since all I have to do is walk away from the mission by myself and someone is sure to follow. It doesn't matter any longer who it is as long as it's a male body. There was a time, when I first arrived, when I thought I could love one of them, but it didn't take long to understand that they themselves were only looking for a quick roll in the jungle with the great big white man.

"Listen to me, my friend, and I'll tell you about tenderness.

"How long does it take for a man to die? how long to live? I've learned to do both right here. Take a headful of Father Moiseis and you'll learn quickly enough to die. Watch him trying to teach about *his* God, *his* ideas of sin and morality. Sometimes I tell myself that I stay here only to let them know that his way is not the only way of white people. But I live out there, those moments with Wancho or Patiachi or Iliku. A finger against my skin and I'm alive again. Shivering, aching. Is it any better back in New York or Paris?

"Tenderness. I thought I was in love with Iliku because he was the first who came to me—the day after I arrived here. It was all God and gentleness and humanity, the reasons I came here in the first place, and that really is what it seemed like with Iliku. God, gentleness, humanity. Not the padre's way. Not the way I had thought of when I came, but so tender. It was as if my body suddenly was freed from chains. A lot of romantic nonsense, maybe, and I don't know what came over me. In the Sahara, in my clothes, in my robe, that is, there was always guilt, but here there was none of that, the feeling was gone. And whatever it is that I thought he also felt for me was never even there. That's what hurt the most. He came out after me twice. The third time, someone else came. Then someone else. And so it's been all these years. Ten years ago, I didn't know a word of the language and therefore couldn't even ask Iliku what happened, if anything. He didn't ignore me after that, or avoid me, and he laughed and poked me. Weeks later, when I'd been through the whole male content of the mission, he came again, beginning the cycle again, and that's the way it is here, and I can tell you that I'm thoroughly alive every time someone, anyone, comes out there after me."

The drums were beating faster now, louder, I think. Even so, it was silent. Iliku was among the dancers, reeling drunk on the masato. He and the others passed before my eyes, but I didn't see them.

All right C, you can take it from there yourself. You will know him better than I do at this point, and I don't want the responsibility. I am going to leave here. You may not have lived like that at the mission in Quintana Roo, but you will know what he's like. What does it mean that you and I talked those hundreds of nights before your conversion? Did it do you any good at all? Did it do me any good? You talked of the evil of your life and there was no solution but in religion. You became a Catholic, and later you too became a lay missionary. What did you feel then? what went through your mind with all those temptations around you? Do you think any of it still is evil, now that you are back to your old life? What did it mean that you were able to resist at the mission, but later fell? All I could think of the night I went to bed after that talk with Manolo was that I was repeating myself. Is he you? Are you he? How many of you are there? Are you all interchangeable? Which others have passed my way without my recognizing them? And who has recognized me?

7

It is time for me to think a bit about this diary. I did think for a while about it last night and it seems that I can't or don't want to give it up. It was easy when I began to write, not knowing exactly what I was going to put down here or how it was going to affect me, mostly because I knew nothing of what would be happening. It was easy then to say that I would send it off across the mountains. Now I jealously want to keep it with me. I want it with me wherever it is that I'm going. Manolo was angry and upset when I finally told him yesterday that I'd be going away in a couple of days, though he must have known that I'd be going away some time soon. Father Moiseis just shrugged his shoulders as if it didn't matter at all, and Hermano smiled. If a day passes, if a life passes, it is only time, and these pages at least are here to reveal me. It will have to be enough for me now. Sit patiently on this table, all of you blank pages, and wait for me to fill you; there's nothing, no one else that I can touch with my self. Friends and enemies, lend me your hearts! Give me a bit of soul to lie with! Take a piece of me, a page, and burn me with the fires of your fingertips! I go because I must, I said to Manolo. "No!" he shouted at me. "No! You come here out of nowhere and you're going into nowhere as if you hadn't existed at all! Who are you and what do you think you're going to do? Walk along and meet a group of gentle people and have an easy time with them? Look at me! Take a good look! What do you think you're going to find that I haven't been able to find?"

We were sitting on rocks with our feet in the river. It was twilight and it began to rain. A relaxed rain, water easing down from the grey sky, sliding along leaves, dampening our skins and clothes, muffling our talk. Wancho came up to us, bow and arrows in hand. "Don Manolo, there are caymans on the river. Will we go hunt them tonight?"

"Good! We'll go after eating!" He got up and took my arm. "What you need is a little excitement. Something to take your mind off yourself."

The rain had turned to a fine drizzle and the air was cool. Wancho was crouching in front of the pharmacy with Imi and Urqi and he touched their shoulders as we came out of the dining room. Manolo motioned for them to wait and he ran up the ladder to his room and returned with his rifle and a flashlight. The others carried bows and arrows.

All was black. Quickly becoming accustomed to the darkness, my eyes picked out the darker shapes of the trees cut out and pasted on the sky, which was somewhat lighter than the jungle. We tripped over stones, walked through mud, all along a very narrow trail over which I had not yet gone, or which didn't look familiar to me at night. There was no sound other than the hushed drizzle and the accidental snap of a twig. Even the night animals and insects seemed to be waiting and watching with us. Wancho, far in the lead, cupped a hand to his mouth and let out a low-keyed whistle, two short notes and a long, then repeated them. We stopped and Manolo took the flashlight and played it along the ink-like river. Slowly the beam wandered and danced over the surface, back and forth, along the bank, where mysterious shapes of trees and grasses shot up and leaves dipped into water.

Silently we walked over the sand, the flashlight always on the water. We walked slowly, crouched, in dead silence. The flashlight picked out a red eye floating on the water, pulling it toward us as we in turn moved toward it. Manolo carefully handed me the lamp, indicating that I was to keep it trained upon the eye. His silhouette knelt on one knee and aimed the rifle. He motioned me to put my arm over his right shoulder and direct the light along the barrel and onto the glowing eye. I stooped over, waiting. Wancho and the others were not to be seen within the area of my vision.

Bang!! Splash!! White foam flew up. A scream, Aieeeee! The shape of a man jumped, feet first, knees bent, into the water. Manolo was yelling, "Be careful! Be careful! It may not be dead!" But the boy was already there, pulling at the tail. The others ran into the water and within seconds they were dragging the alligator onto the sand. All three were shouting. Fingers went into the bullet hole in the head. They opened their own mouths, opened the great jaws of the alligator, put their fingers back into the bullet-hole, touched the rifle, patted it, stroked it, laughed, jumped up and down, hugged Manolo, hugged me, took off their soaked trousers and threw them into the water, letting them float away without a thought, and hugged each other in turn.

Manolo was exhilarated and was ready to go for another. It had stopped raining and a piece of moon came out from behind a cloud. "Oh, oh. There's a distracting element. But we'll try anyway." The dead alligator, lit up by the moon, lay on the sand as if ready to snap an arm.

Farther along, the water covered the beach and the bottom fell lower and lower. We waded up to our ribs before it shallowed again to shore. Once more the stillness, the flashlight inching over a currentless pool, a section of the river. The moon hid itself behind a black gash of cloud, returning us to the somber blackness. Another red eye materialized, lured to the ray of light, the bait that led to death. There was the same sequence of silence, the same burst from the rifle, the same splash into the water of the men and the quick dragging out of the creature, again dead with the first shot.

"Christ! but this is my lucky night. Usually I miss— and this is a damned big one, twelve or thirteen feet. We should celebrate! Dance a little and drink some masato, if we had it."

We each took an appendage and pulled and floated the alligator to where we had left the first one. We were all delighted with the night's work, particularly Manolo, who could not stop smiling and laughing. Even in all the dampness of the day's rain, a fire was built in the open, and Manolo and I took off our shirts and trousers and we sat close to the flames and warmed our bodies.

Manolo got up and stretched, sending a shiver through his body. He lay down and rested his head on Wancho's thigh. "Where are you going, my friend? Isn't this a moment of life? A moment to live again and again? They may not love you, whatever that may mean, but they want you here with them. Haven't we shared in death? in the hunt? What more do you want?"

8

The excitement of these weeks that have gone by has increased to such a degree that I no longer have the will or strength to allow another day to pass without expelling some of that energy into this diary.

I left the mission with no more than a wave to Father Moiseis, Hermano, and the Indians. Manolo put his hands on my shoulders. "Ciao," is all he said, as if I were to return the next day. Wancho and Alejo were waiting by one of the rafts with my knapsack and food, to take me across the river. I waved again, for the last time. The only thing I said myself was, Goodbye, when I left the two Puerangas on the other side.

Even so, it was an eloquent, unspoken parting. The clamminess of fear within me at that final break with everything that was part of my recent past, remote past, of all my known life, of everything experienced by my body and mind, was not generated by what lay ahead. Time that is to come and what happens to me within it are speculations that can be invoked only through the whole of myself, within the context of my thought and existence, and limited by all that I have fed into me. So my fears were not so much for the future but for what I left behind. Not for the people or places, but for my knowledge. I was cutting away all that I knew about myself, I was removing my own reflection, and as I walked on, I walked into an incarnation of myself that had always been there, so hidden it had never reached the outer layers of my soul. I lived then, during those few days, in each hour and each day, and they enclosed me like the forest itself. Time separated itself into fragments, each one discarded to make way for my emerging self. Not like those other days when I walked to the mission, when time was fused and exhilarating, but I was allowing my secrets to come forth, shedding the disguise that I had never known was only a screen. I did not look for the Indians now; I simply transferred myself toward them. There were no pictures in my mind of what they would look like, no ideas of what their reactions might be.

It was the fourth day and I was walking along munching on fried bits of yuca that I had soaked in a stream to soften, and I came out from among a huddle of bushes to a long rocky beach, at the far end of which, against a solid wall of green, some spots of red attracted my eye. My first thought was that they must be blossoms of some kind that I had never seen before, but they were too much like solid balls, and they moved slightly, though there wasn't the slightest breeze. A few steps farther on I frowned and shook my head, wondering even more what they could be and then it came over me in a shiver that these spots were faces, and they were all turned in my direction, all unmoving. Still closer, I made out a group of men, their bodies variously painted in black and red, looking tiny against the gigantic backdrop of the jungle that stretched so high above them. No one moved; no one turned his eyes away or looked anywhere but straight at me. They were frozen in place. They were squatting tightly together, chins on knees, arms on one another's shoulders, leaning over resting heads upon another's knee, or thigh or flank. They continued to stare, moving neither a toe nor an eyelash. Smiles were fixed upon their faces, mouths were closed, placid. Some had match-like sticks through their lower lips, others had bone through noses. Their feet and toes curled round stones and twigs in the same way that their hands held vertically bows and long arrows, and axes of stone tied to short pieces of bough. Long, well-combed bangs ran over their foreheads into the scarlet paint of their faces and hair covered the length of their backs and shoulders. Masses of necklaces of seeds and huge animal teeth and small yellow and black birds hung down from thick necks and almost touched the stones between their open thighs.

Still no one moved as I approached. There were thirteen, fifteen of them, I never knew. Off to one side, on the right, without ever taking my eyes from the men, I was able to see two fires burning in front of two small structures of branches and leaves, and I felt rather than saw figures lying within. I came up to the men, stood but a few feet away. Still no one moved, still no one made a gesture of any kind, no gesture of hate or love, no gesture of curiosity or fear. My feet moved, my arm went out automatically and I put a hand easily upon the nearest shoulder, and I smiled. The head leaned over and briefly rested its cheek upon my hand, almost caressing it. The body got up, straightening out, and the frozen smile split open and laughter came out, giggles at first, then great bellows that echoed back against the wall of trees. He threw his arms around me, almost crushing with strength and pleasure, the laughter continuing, doubling, trebling, until I realized that all the men had got up and were laughing and embracing each other, holding their bellies as if in pain, rolling on the ground with feet kicking the air. All weapons had been left lying on stones and we were jumping up and down and my arms went around body after body and I felt myself getting hysterical, wildly estatic with love for all humanity, and I returned slaps on backs and bites on hard flesh, and small as they were, I twirled some round like children and wept away the world of my past.

A pair of claw-like hands, black with paint as if they had gloves on them, suddenly were pulling at my shirt, pulling it apart at the neck and buttons popped, while other hands were stretching out the waist of my trousers and I felt a head pushing into my stomach as its eyes tried to look down and a hand went in and scratched my thigh and cupped my testicles and penis. My sneakers were pulled off by someone below me, and he took hold of the legs of my trousers and pushed them up as high as they would go. A handkerchief came out of my pocket and soon covered a head. More hands went into pockets and found a box of matches, which opened by itself and the matchsticks scattered over the ground. We all bent to pick them up and they were removing similar sticks from their lower lips and replacing them with these when a flash of flame appeared between my hands and shrieks of astonishment went up and long whispers of Ooooo-oooooo and two fingers reached out and closed themselves on the fire and a shout of pain gave it reality, and they backed away an instant but returned and I lit another. Ooooo-oooooo, they whispered, and from a lower lip came a match that was examined carefully and the man hit it on the top of the box and broke it in two. Another tried and again it broke in two. I showed them where to strike the match and they looked at me and uttered low clicking sounds.

From behind me someone had finally pulled out my shirttails and was pushing the shirt up and pinching my skin, then rubbing it with the flat of his palm. A cold tongue licked at my back and then came around to my hand and licked again. I unbuttoned the last of the buttons on my shirt and took it off. I removed my trousers. Hands were all over me again, pulling hard at the hair on my chest, pulling at the hair of my groin, lifting my penis and whispering Ooooo-oooooo, spreading the cheeks of my buttocks, and hugging, always hugging me. They each had a turn at touching my whole body, and some came up and held their penises alongside mine, comparing them. My nipples ached from the pinching and it seemed that my body hair would soon be removed, painfully. At

last we all squatted down and they spoke to me as if
I understood their language fluently.

This was the beginning of my meeting with the
Akaramas, and now, living within their lives, I have
become what I have always been and it has taken a
lifetime, all of my own life, to reach this point where
it is as if I know finally that I am alive and that I am
here, right now. I have thought back often to that
meeting, to when I first knew that those shapes were
human, that they were men who had killed other humans and had eaten their flesh, that they were the
first men who had ever walked upon the earth, and
that my own world, whatever, wherever it was, no
longer was anywhere in existence. I walk alone, and
have always walked alone. I have walked this time,
this last time, where my legs took me, as if the nerves
of my body all extended in the one direction that
would take me here. In writing, I think. That is, in
writing here, it has become necessary to put thoughts
together that go down on these pages. But when I
walk, I am driven in some inexplicable way, almost as
if the way were one I had traveled before, and I put
my foot down on crunching leaves, lift the other leg
and place the foot forward, stepping where it has always known it would step again. And coming upon
my people, now my lovers, my friends, I shed my past
as I did my clothes, even knowing inside me that I
could never be a Michii or Yoreitone, that a shirt,
though gone now in shreds, though it no longer is an

object for which I have any desire or need, remains forever something that I know has somewhere a use, and I can never strip myself of the knowledge of how to open a button, how to put my arms in sleeves, how to put the tails inside a pair of pants. To become Michii, I must not only rid myself of the need to write, but also of the very knowledge that writing exists. Whatever self I have opened within me is one which forever must retain a sense of another world. In my hand at this moment is a pen and it is making marks on paper. On my hand is the black paint that comes from the fruit of the huito tree. There are designs painted over my body and I have scraped away with a bone knife all hair below my shoulders. So I sit here writing, naked. Was I in the same way naked before them, before I had removed my shirt and trousers? Had I bared my soul before my body? How is it that they did not kill me? How is it that I was not frightened of them? Again it is questions, and questions without answers. They were there, squatting in front of mahogany trees and the picture of them registered itself upon my brain, clicking like a camera, and there were no thoughts, nothing to tell me to be afraid, that they are cannibals, but it's as if I absorbed them through my flesh, an osmosis whereby they came into me, into me, inside me, ran along with my bloodstream, became white and red corpuscles, the air that entered me, the food of my gullet and stomach, crept along my dermis like a second skin. They entered into my pores. What smell did I exude that allowed them to accept me? It was in Borneo that Mathurin Daim had said, "You are the only Westerner whose smell I have ever been able to bear." There, I knew well that having lived for so long among his people, eating their foods, my body smells were like his own. But here, it is something else, something to do with the fact that I came as I did, that I came alone and in need. I knew that they recognized me, that we recognized each other. We played games and hugged each other. My skin was white and they licked it to see if the paint would come off and were pleased when it remained its strange color. Time after time they ran their hands over my chest and belly and penis. They touched with gentle fingers my nose, my eyes, my ears, my hair, and they prodded into my navel with their noses. They repeated one word over and over, Habe, habe, and it has taken me all this time to understand its meaning: "ignorant one."

It might be that an hour passed and they were still talking to me, and all I could do was shake my head and nod as thoughts of what they might be saying went through my mind. Some of the men stood before me on one leg, resting the other foot on its calf. Perhaps from the very first I knew that they were naked, but it was only later that I looked at them, realized that they wore only paint, and began to some extent to study the designs on their bodies. Some men had a band of black around the waist, buttocks, and sexual parts, as if wearing shorts or bathing suits, and their hair was clipped in crew-cut fashion with a pigtail running down the nape of the neck. Slightly older men, though they too were young, had clean thin paint lines going down from below the neck to the knees, with a design from chest to groin of double inverted vees. The youngest boys were completely black, though their faces too were scarlet. One man seemed out of place; his body was splashed and splattered with red and black as if he were the beginning of a Jackson Pollock. Everyone's hands and feet were black with gloves and shoes. No one looked more than twenty-two.

We were all squatting there, knitted together, and I was talking and laughing, telling them, only because of a need to talk back, whether they understood or not, all about the mission and about my life in New York, when a woman appeared from one of the lean-tos. She could have been fourteen or eighteen. She had small breasts that stood out straight from her chest. She covered her face with one hand and with the other held out a piece of meat. Her hair was cut very short and she was black from neck to toe, except for the upper chest, which was carefully painted in spots of red to form a vee that ended just above her navel. Her face remained hidden until a man took the meat and she turned back to the shelter.

Beside one of the shelters, a large monkey was being cooked over a smoking fire. From the coals, long tubes of yuca stuck out. The sun had gone down and I became silent and listening. Whispers filled the cool night air. A wind brushed against the forest and leaves swayed and rustled. Figures around the fire moved in slow motion as if nudged along by this tranquil breeze. Three other women tended the fire and meat. The oldest carried a baby on her back, wrapped in leaves and vines. They did not look in my direction. The man who I came later to know as Michii (for it was weeks before I knew anyone's name) and who was sitting behind me with his thighs against the sides of my body, so close up that I could rest my elbows on his knees, poked me on the back and I turned around. He was chewing on a piece of the monkey meat, masticating it without seeming to swallow. He opened his mouth and let the meat fall into his hand and held it out to me. A little unsure, I took it, put it into my own mouth, chewed and swallowed. He laughed and tilted his head and then gave me the charred arm from which he had been eating. The singed hairs of the animal stood up like thorns all over it. I bit into the flesh and blood and juice ran out. It was tough, stringy, unsalted, delicious. Michii took a banana from a stalk that had just been dropped there beside him and sank his teeth into the skin, bit along it quickly to split the peel, and with a quick movement, tore it apart and pushed the whole fruit into his mouth. He peeled another and gave it to me, pushing it into my mouth with his own hands. After we had eaten several bananas he reached behind him for a long section of sugar cane, broke it over the top of his head into short lengths, and handed one to me. His front teeth were short and arched, filed down from biting into the hard outer layer of the cane. Each time he handed me something to eat, he said "Baapendée."

I slept intermittently that night, on leaves and bodies and branches. At dawn we breakfasted on more yuca and monkey meat, and when all stomachs were full, all food and weapons were gathered together and we set off into the jungle. I had no idea where we were going. My clothes had disappeared, but I found my knapsack untouched and managed to remove, from the feet of two different men, my sneakers.

Well, Manolo, where are you and what do you say now? "They are fattening you up for the kill," you will think. But I did not feel that, and here I lie on my stomach on the ground, with three young men leaning on me watching each movement of the pen.

9

We walked all that morning and part of the afternoon. There were no rest stops. There were some abrupt pauses to listen to bird and animal sounds, to look at prints in the mud, and twice two men went off on their own and brought back an armadillo, alive, two wild turkeys, and an ocelot, which I expected would be for our supper. We had to cross the same river many times, always having to swim it, and it wound in so many directions that I had no idea how far we traveled, except that we were always going east. We might have gone into Bolivia or into Brazil. The woman with the baby on her back floated across those stretches of river as if she were resting on a log. Sometime in the afternoon we came back to the water but did not go across. Instead we stopped and the women built a small fire and all the men and women set about the business of repainting themselves, since so much of the color on their bodies had faded, washed off in the rivers we had crossed.

Huito is a grey fruit, the size of a large orange. It was held down on a flat stone and pounded with another stone for about half an hour, softening it, and then was put into the ashes of the fire for about ten minutes. A hole was made in one end and a clear, transparent juice was squeezed into a gourd. The liquid, in this almost completely transparent condition, was brushed onto the body with a flat piece of wood, or was simply rubbed on with both hands if the area to be covered was large. They painted themselves and each other. About an hour later, the designs began to darken. The scarlet paint was an easier affair and came from the thistled pod of the achiote bush, which has seeds inside that turn red when squashed between the palms, and this is then rubbed onto their faces.

By the time they were ready to cross the river, the sun was already resting on top of the forest. A short walk and an enormous house rose up in a clearing. People were sitting outside and they looked up at us, older men with thick bands of black from shoulder to knee. They got up slowly and stood there. Michii went over and there was whispering and embracing, then smiles, and they all came up to me and said, "Habe. Habe, habe."

There were no buildings around but this one great hut, more than a hundred feet long and about twenty feet wide, twelve feet high. Smoke seeped through the roof. From a small hole at one end, men, women, children crawled out by the dozens to look at me and though the hilarity of the meeting on the rocky beach was not repeated, they emanated a feeling of warmth to which I responded with open arms. An old man motioned us to enter the hut and I knelt on all fours and crawled inside. Dense smoke hovered in the air, rising slowly to escape through cracks in the roof. I coughed and tears came to my eyes. A long series of fires ran in file down the center, and along the sides were low partitions of branches, no more than two feet high, that formed compartments. There were bows and arrows everywhere, leaning against walls, and fiber carrying bags and gourds hanging down, knives and axes lay in corners or were set between the bark that formed the wall, bunches of bananas and pineapple and yuca and cuts of meat were strung from beams, and there was a litter of twigs, leaves, fruit skins and cores, feathers, wood shavings, feces, animal bones and skins, through all of which hopped and shrieked small monkeys and parrots and other birds. Michii was immediately behind me and he pulled me by the hand, running half the length of the hut, to between partitions and pushed me down and sat himself and laughed.

Within seconds the hut came to life as everyone crawled in and the men sat while the women with crying babies on their backs stoked fires and children ran up and down, all half visible to me in the haze of smoke. The whole inside wall of the hut, where the compartments were, seemed filled with men, and all the women and children remained within the center area tending the fires and cooking. Later, I learned that this was normal and that only on rare occasions did the men and women sleep side by side inside the hut. In the back of the section in which I sat with Michii and Darinimbiak, with Reindude, Baaldore and Ihuene, where the roof sloped to the ground, was

a log that ran from partition to partition, that we used
as a bench and at night turned into a pillow for the
six of us, or for those whose heads did not have the
advantage of resting upon a soft abdomen. An old man
came up to us and squatted down. There was a hole
where one eye was missing and his face had deep
wrinkles as if cut in with a knife. His name was Yoreitone, he said. He was the chief, and he had come to
me now to tell me how happy he was at my arrival. I
did not need to understand his speech to know what
it was he was saying. The expressions on his face, the
movements of his hands, and the tone of his whispered
words were enough. It is only weeks now that I have
been here, but I can translate his words. "You have
come a long way and you will rest with us. You have
come a long way and you will rest with us. We are
content that you have come and you will remain."
Now I can answer, "I have come a long way and I
am happy to rest with you." The welcoming sentences
were repeated over and over, and finally Yoreitone sat
amongst us, with an arm on the shoulder of Michii
and another around the waist of Ihuene.

Food was brought by several women, each carrying
fruit or meat on leaves, which were set in front of us.
Michii waited for Yoreitone to pick his piece of meat,
picked up one for himself, and began to whisper. I
watched his face and gestures, and his whispering had
such a quality of conveying life and form that even
then I felt I understood his every phrase. He told the
story of our meeting in such complex detail that it
must have been two hours, even more, until I had

even removed my clothing and stood before them naked. He described me completely, perhaps even my every thought, as I sat there next to him listening, and hands touched and stroked me to confirm his impressions. It could not have been a straight narrative, because it seemed to weave back and forth in time, and within it all he told of every bird he had seen, moving his arms slowly in great sweeps of flight, and he told how the leaves fell from trees with quivering movements of fingers, how a river turned its bend, how deep it was, its color, and the color of the sky at each moment of the day, the direction of the wind and how it moved light branches and leaves, and somewhere then I fell asleep with his hand on my cheek, waking briefly at times during the night to see the women round the fires feeding logs into the flames with their agile toes, falling asleep again to the color and rhythm of Michii's voice, which went on and on through the darkness into the same darkness and heavy smoke that remained in the hut while dawn lit up the world outside.

10

How much time, for how many weeks, have I been here? The moon can tell me, I know, yet I look at the moon only for itself, for the light by which I walk, for the glow it sets within me as I lie on leaves. Ooooo-ooooo, it whispers, and Ooooo-ooooo I whisper back.

The day came when I started to sketch and it began one morning because Darinimbiak brought me two little green parrots while I was still asleep, still wrapped together with Reindude. He sat on my stomach to wake me up and let his long hair drip down onto my face. His body sparkled with drops of dew from the forest. His face shone, and his eyes threw off a light that blinded. He sat there a while with the parrots noisily cupped against his chest and he told how he had found them in a nest, pausing between sentences to take out the stick that was in his lower lip and pushing his tongue into the hole to force out trickles of saliva. He put the stick back and laughed, talked another sentence, took the stick out again and played with it. He took up the birds and held them both on a finger, securing them there with a thumb. He put a piece of yuca in his mouth, chewed it, puckered out his lips, opened the beak of one parrot with his other hand and stuffed some of the softened yuca into it with his tongue. He did the same with the other bird, then handed them both to me. He showed me how to tie a leg with fiber string and we built a nest in a corner with leaves that were scattered near the fire.

Darinimbiak crouched over the coals and pulled out more yuca, testing each one to make sure it was done. We ate by the fire and I got up and took out pen, ink, and paper, and began to draw. Darinimbiak moved up, took the paper from me, turned it over, tore it, took the pen and began to chew the wood, then the nib. Reindude and others were already around me. I pushed Darinimbiak and arranged him in what I hoped was a comfortable position, with him frowning at me in wonder, and I motioned for him to sit still, and I began again. Someone sat on my shoulder, someone pushed my arm, someone took the pen and pushed it through the paper several times and everyone laughed at the holes. I laughed with them and tore the sheet into small bits and threw them up into the air like confetti. I forced everyone to sit down and I whispered in English telling them what it was I was trying to do. Two women were sitting at the next fire arranging coals, while children slept in their laps undisturbed by their mothers' movements. Lines appeared on my paper, almost the whole of the head of one of the women, when she turned to see me staring at her. She rolled on her buttocks and thighs, moving herself until I saw only her back. The other woman got up and put herself down next to her, tightly against her, a Siamese twin. Again I started, with bodies leaning on me, hands upon my drawing hand. Darinimbiak stood directly in front of me and bent down to touch his nose against my nose and stayed there until I was cross-eyed and gently moved him from my line of vision. His head was suddenly in my lap and he was staring up at me with an ear-to-ear smile on his face. I got up and put my things away and we all laughed and hugged and Darinimbiak took me around the waist and led me out of the hut.

In the afternoon, I went out alone with my sketching material and walked into the forest and did detailed drawings of the foliage. It was the first time I had been alone at all and three or four times, while I sat on a tree trunk drawing, I heard voices calling, but I did not answer them. When I got back, it was as if I had not been away at all, as though no one had gone out to call me. Women were carrying bananas and stalks of sugar cane into the hut. Outside, Michii, Baaldore, and Darinimbiak were sitting on a log scraping down bows and arrows, shaping the points with the tooth of a nutria set into monkey bone. I showed them the two drawings I had done and they turned them around, turned them over, crumpled them, laughing, always laughing. Michii went back to his scraping and again my pen was making lines. This time what I was doing did not seem to interest them, and I finished what I think is a good sketch of Michii. He looked at it and returned to his arrow. Darinimbiak and Baaldore also looked and pointed out the designs on Michii's body and the designs on my drawing, tracing them with my pen, but they could not seem to understand. There are now seven drawings among my things.

It had been only the day before that we had learned each other's names. Yoreitone had told me his on my first day, for he acted not only as chief but as a kind of witch doctor as well, and it was only he whose name I was told. Among all the words that I had heard pouring from their half-opened lips in whispers, there might have been the names of Michii or Darinimbiak or others. Or at night as we lay together, they might have called to one another. But a name or a word would have been the same to me during those earliest days when I knew nothing of the language. There had been no indication that they wished to know my own name, but on that day Michii and I had breakfast together and Ihuene was passing through the hut, carrying a hand of bananas, and Michii whispered, "Ihuene!" Ihuene looked at him and whispered, "Michii!" and he stopped a second or two and whispered again, "Michii!" It was a moment that I understood was full of meaning and Michii paled and put a nervous finger on my thigh. With his other hand, he covered his mouth, uncovered it and whispered, "Michii!" His hand reached over and cupped itself over my own mouth and when he removed it, I whispered out my own name.

Ihuene had gone. The hut was empty of everyone but ourselves and the pet birds and animals. Fires were low, and smoke rested in the air above them like a grey cloud. Michii stood and pulled me up and we crawled out of the hut and walked into the forest. He built a small fire and then stood in front of it with his arms stretched out and he called a name, a word, "Bidire!" He shouted, "Bidire!" in a voice louder than any I'd heard before and the look on his face was of anger. Again he shouted out "Bidire!" and stamped on the fire with a bare foot. He found a stone and beat the embers until all that remained was charred wood, no longer smoking. We returned to the hut and Michii sat and talked, and I understood then that names were told only to friends, for names could be shouted in the forest and used for magical purposes. That night I learned the names of all those in our compartment.

I have been walking around barefoot since the day I got here and calluses instead of cuts are beginning to form. It seemed ridiculous to me to go around naked and have sneakers on my feet.

The thought of nakedness did not occur to me until I saw a young woman making a garment of leaves. She tied a batch of these into a kind of skirt and wrapped it around her waist and thighs. She walked to the river, floated her way across, returned a few minutes later and then dropped the skirt at the water's edge. The carelessness, the inattention with which she discarded the leaves, brought back into my mind the first time I had seen a naked woman. When I was young, thirteen or fourteen, I went, against my father's wishes, to a WPA art school on Union Street in Brooklyn. I had heard of naked models, had seen forbidden photos of them, yet somehow it was never anything that I would see myself, nothing that could become a part of my life. When I sat there in class on that first summer day a young woman came out from behind a screen wrapped in a robe, it seemed impossible that she would stand up on that platform and drop the robe. She took it off, I flushed, blood pounded in my head and I trembled and felt that every eye in the room was turned on me. Casually, I hoped casually, I got up and went to the window and breathed in deeply. Some minutes later, I sat down on my stool, looked straight at the model, picked up my piece of charcoal and began to draw.

It is a strange and surprising way of life here, and I am always learning and seeing new things. About half the women are pregnant. The other day I was out sketching. As I was coming back I saw one of these women alone digging a hole at the edge of a field. She knelt over the hole, her knees wide apart. She let out a groan and a great wet mass dropped down. She sang a long, high-pitched note and another woman came and knelt with her. The mother picked up the baby and they filled in the hole. I followed them to the river, where they washed the child and then took up the body of a small jaguar which had been lying there and allowed the blood from its slit throat to drip down onto the infant's head. They went back to the hut, passing by my three friends with bows and arrows without nodding to them. Later, I saw her working at the fire with the baby asleep in a cradle on her back.

I lay down in my compartment with the other men, thinking of the sketches I had done and watching Michii brush his hair with a densely thistled pod. Darinimbiak began to giggle and slapped Michii on the back and thighs and took up his penis and pulled at it and caressed the testicles. He leaned over and slapped my leg, pulled at the end of my penis and pointed to the woman who had given birth that afternoon and shoved at Michii's back, and hugged him from behind, telling me that Michii had become a father. Michii himself gave no sign of pride or pleasure, and though the mother and child were no more than ten feet away, at the edge of the nearest fire, he made no move toward them. After we had eaten, he got up and went out, passing his child on the way, glancing down for only an instant.

We live apart here, the men and the women. There are children and pregnancies. Yet in the middle of the night no one moves from his partition to seek out a partner. A partner is there next to you, huddled up to you, arms and legs around you.

11

Last night, after we came back from a hunting trip, Michii presented me with a bow and six arrows of two types, four wide-bladed bamboo arrows for animals like monkeys and ocelots, and two made of ebony with notched shafts and sharpened ends, for birds. This morning he and Darinimbiak led me out to a field and began to teach me how to use them. I had thought that the day they both sat me by the river and painted me with the same designs they wore themselves, the day also that Michii scraped off the hair on my body, for the first time, with a nutria's tooth, that somehow I had then, with no other ceremony, become a member of the tribe, had become within that short time as close as possible to being an Akarama, to accepting myself as the being I had always dreamt myself to be. Until the bow and arrows were offered, they gave me everything: laughter, food, themselves, time; but with that presentation came also the need to learn their use, a sympathy for the weapons themselves, as if without them it was only my mind that lived here and my body, even with all its pleasures, had remained in other worlds. But oh! what a fiasco I made of that first lesson! I tried pulling the bow, and I pulled and I pulled and I stretched it out a foot and a half. I fitted an arrow and it jumped away. Michii and Darinimbiak rolled with laughter. Darinimbiak's arms came around me and together we shot an arrow into the air, straight up, and it hung there a moment, resting before turning its head and dropping at our feet. Again my arrow flipped away, again the bow made only a slight arch. There was no impatience as time passed, only a lessening of the laughter, and I improved and finally was able to send an arrow straight and somewhat close to its hoped-for distance. For me it was as if I had conquered an earthly element, and there was a glow on their faces that held me staring from one to the other until they placed the bow and arrows in my hand and back we went to the hut and lay down to sleep, one upon the other.

We went off the other morning, yesterday it was, as if we were going for a swim in the river or into the edge of the jungle to find an edible bird or two. The three of us, Michii and Darinimbiak and I, suddenly were inside the forest racing along as if we were already on the track of some great animal. I looked down at my bare feet with shock and pleasure as they moved along, those feet of mine, and trod upon the ground, upon the twigs and debris, with no uncertainty, without the pains of cuts that had been so habitual, and had seemed then to be a part of my feet themselves. We stopped and they examined leaves and earth and sniffed the air, and on we went, slower.

There was another time five or six years ago, when

the sky was the rose of that painting I sold to C, and I was following a Murut in Borneo, over a hunting trail. He carried a blowgun in his hand, there was a bone through the bun of his hair, and we were racing along the way we are now, with leeches on my legs and no time then to brush them off as he stopped an instant to bend and test the tiny footprints for their moistness and off again we went, slower then, slowing down to an absolute silence on a still evening with the air as clear as it can ever be, and the long tube moved up to his mouth and flutt! the dart flew out through leaves and branches, moving them along its path, and suddenly his voice screeching as he rushed back towards me, a mouse deer slung across his shoulder. I ran a hand over its fur and the Murut touched a finger on my breast and pointed into the trees above us and there, staring down, were three orangutans. And still another time, when C was touching me and pointing up into the jungle of Chiapas and three Lacandon Indians stood there in the trees in their dirty shifts, three arrows in their three drawn bows aimed in our direction.

Suddenly again a hand was on my arm pointing. Michii's hand, pointing to a large grey animal rushing wildly through the brush. We ran on and came to deep water, into which the animal jumped and almost hid itself, only a snout and ears above the surface. An arrow, two arrows, three, splashed the water behind the snout. Michii and Darinimbiak were swimming before I knew they had moved. They reached the already dead animal and floated it back to shore.

Out of the water, the huge tapir took on a brownish color. Michii took hold of its snout and wiggled it back and forth and laughed. With the long, sharp edge of one of his bamboo arrows, Darinimbiak sliced through the underside and removed the innards, carrying them into the river to clean. Michii cut away at the head and soon had it separated from the body. He searched out two thick branches, sharpened an end of each, staked the head on one and ran the second through the animal's body. After that first laughter, we made no other sounds but looked at one another often with smiles as they worked and I watched and helped when it was possible. The innards were wrapped in leaves and tied with vines to the stake that held the head and this was given to me to carry, while they lifted the immense creature onto their shoulders and began to trot their way back to the hut. It was dark when we reached our village. We crawled through the entrance hole, dragging the tapir behind us. Michii took the head to Yoreitone, who immediately set it onto the coals of a fire. Darinimbiak opened the package of innards, held up the liver and ran to the fire in front of the area in which we slept and began to roast it, holding it over the heat with a long stick. The rest of the animal was cut up into small pieces and distributed among all the others. My shoulder ached where I had held the head and I lay down between Baaldore and Ihuene, who pressed themselves up close and asked about our trip. I whispered out my story, moving my hands and body in description, varying my tone for color, and they were hearing me, listening to me, imitating my gestures to gather into themselves what I was saying, in this way making it more clear to themselves, and though my words in their language were few, my movements were long and changing and as my arms stretched out a bow and an arrow flew, their eyes widened with interest and fascination as they knew it would reach its target. It was not a long story I told, and Michii might have taken two hours to tell it, but it pleased me so to tell this tale and I was feeling more than ever part of this family. Darinimbiak came over as I was finishing my last descriptive movement. He already had in his mouth the pierced liver, biting off a piece to give me. It melted in my mouth.

12

I was feeling confident in my new language when an evening came that Yoreitone sat outside the hut upon a jaguar skin, surrounded by boys of twelve or fourteen. His parrot-feathered mace lay in his lap. His face was clear of paint, but black lines circled his neck, beginning at the chin and continuing into the strands of jaguar teeth that hung down to his navel, and also covered his upper arms. Wide bands of black reached from his clavicle to his knees, while thinner lines followed the contours of his thighs and calves. His testicles but not his penis were also black and a line ran from there, passing over the anus up to the coccyx, where it ended in a long filled-in inverted vee. He had the match-like stick in his lower lip. All of the boys were painted exactly alike, black from chin to toe, scarlet on their faces.

Yoreitone stretched an arm up to the moon, paused in his whispering until I had settled among them, and continued, "And then you will have the woman and you will see what you must do with her. You have heard our speaking and you know what you must do, and you have seen. The fruit is ready." The boys nodded slowly, expressions of understanding on their faces. I waited for Yoreitone to go on and explain further. He shifted his body off to one side by rolling his thighs and buttocks, sat up in a squat, and defecated loudly, then moved back onto the skin. He did not speak again, but no one left the circle.

I opened my mouth and uttered a sound, hesitated, and then at an opening gesture from Yoritone, his palms up, spreading out his fingers and his arms, I asked in my own whisper, "Tell me, Old One. Tell me from where do men come?"

He patted my forearm and laughed. "You are very ignorant." The boys giggled into their hands as if a great tension had been released, but they stopped as Yoreitone lifted his head, lifted and rattled his mace, replaced it in his lap, and nodded his head up and down several times.

"So you do not know that all men come from the heights? Yes, it was many times ago, many, many times of death ago, that we were all living up there." He pointed the mace toward the sky and moved it as if to encompass the whole of the heavens.

"One day an opening split through the heights and men in wonder came from everywhere to look at it. They looked down from the hole that had split and they liked what they saw. There was light, and there were rivers with fishes in them and under the trees were many animals to hunt, and they wanted to go down. But they had not enough rope to reach to the bottom, and much time, a great deal of time, each day they all worked, and time went by while they made the rope long enough, because the heights were so high that even the strongest arm could not send an arrow to reach them. And when they finished making the rope, they climbed down and began to eat of the hunt and of the fishes of the rivers. But the spirits from above became angry because we had left them and they were all alone and man was not with them. It began to rain and the waters of the rivers boiled, and the men, in order not to be drowned or burned, went out to look for the tall, tall tree, the huamée, it was called, so they could take refuge there and they could live and eat, and also the animals lived in the tree with them. Also the jaguar and his woman, and mama the crocodile too. It was a long time that they lived there, and when there was no longer so much water, some of the men wanted to go down from the tree, but the waters were still hot and it killed them. And later others went down and then there was no water and there were no fires. Then the mukas, the wild pigs, came down, and these were the first that man ate, and last of all came down the jaguar and his woman. But this was many times ago, many times of death ago, and no one knows where this huamée tree is. We look for it when we go into the forest, but always it hides from us, but a time will come to find it."

Here he was, Yoreitone, my chief, sitting and telling me a story and looking at me with his one eye as he looked upon his family, his body full of gentleness, a finger now and then resting on my knee, and when he had finished the tale and sat there simply within the aura of its meaning, with no movement of any kind, it was as if he had opened his arms to welcome a child to his breast, and I cannot help but wonder who this man is, with his wrinkled face and eye that speaks to all of past and future, and I cannot help but wonder where within him lay the murder of that family that sent Wassen to the mission. Once, in childhood, an old man with a skull cap covering a bald patch, and a long grey beard with curls at its ends, used to sit at a kitchen table in the back of my father's grocery store, teaching in Hebrew the Five Books of Moses. With each of my mistakes he cracked a thumb and finger on my head, and I left those books forever with no feeling for God, but only full of stories that talked of vengeance, hate, and war. Yoreitone, within my hearing, had not yet talked of death or war, but always he told of hunting trips for monkeys and birds, and other creatures that lived and stalked within the forest, tales of spirits that inhabited deer to feed the jaguar and therefore could not be tracked to kill, and tales that wandered in time and space and seemed to me no legend or symbol but did no more than tell of walks to new rivers and trees. Later, I asked Yoreitone what he thought of the white upon the mountains far in the distance, the mountains that could only be seen on the clearest of days, the mountains that reached up to twenty thousand feet and more. "Flowers," he said. "They are white flowers."

Tell me again, Manolo, the words of Wassen. Tell me how he found them dead. Tell me now the hands that killed were those of Yoreitone and of Michii. I walk within my world a man, I think, and every day confirms my need to live it out with all my senses, not like you, Manolo, living only the moments of the days for which you said you waited. My friends are real and solid, to be slapped and bitten, friends to race with along the jungle floor to shoot an arrow into food. What did you say to me the night before I left? We will both of us die here, deep in a jungle we grow around ourselves. No day of death has yet entered me and I see my friends as proof of my own aliveness, no reflection of them, but a response all my own that wakes me up with no alarm ringing in my ears and takes me through the day with no dream thoughts to tell me what I hope will come. Michii's face is round, his eyes are always narrowed with a squint or a smile, his head of hair is blown by wind and filled with bits of dried leaf, his lips are thin, his body straight from shoulder to hip, and his thighs widen with muscle. Darinimbiak's smile is sad and thoughtful, there's a hint of a mustache above his heavy lips, his bangs are cut often, to keep them well above his eyebrows, and each night he brushes his hair before we lie down to sleep. Baaldore is thick and square, with eyes and mouth wide open, a belly button protruding from a protruding belly, hair tied back with fiber, a small nose and an almost flat face. Reindude is always splashed with red and black, his body and his cheeks, and his face is the squarest of all the men; his nose is widest, sometimes it has a bone inside it; and his bangs are longest. Ihuene is the most elegant. He arranges his hair in a mirror of water. His cheekbones are high and his nostrils are small in the perfectly straight, short nose. All eyes are the same color of brown, all hair the same black, and all the men stand about five feet five, small for ease and speed inside the jungle. The others too have their individuality, but these I know best, having sketched them most, having spent each night sleeping against the textures of their skin. It would not be right to say their personalities are as various as their faces, nor is it possible to say they are all the same. Michii is a maker of quick decisions, Darinimbiak is always eating and searches out palm shoots each time we go into the forest, Baaldore loves birds and has taken over the feeding of my parrots, Reindude is a follower and never goes anywhere alone, and Ihuene frowns and ponders an hour after daylight before he thinks of a plan for the day, as if the day had need of plans.

The women, then, had been by the river for two days, making large clay pots and drying them in the sun. They brought small, ripe pineapples from a field where they grew with yuca and peanuts and wild bushes. They cut the fruit apart, chewed it, and spit the juice into the clay pots and threw away the pulp. The juice leaked out through cracks that were then stopped up with more clay. The pots were covered with leaves and left in the shade another day. Morning came. Michii got up and brought me a bowl of the fermenting juice, very sour and tasting of the clay. We ate no other food. There were fires outside and

Yoreitone sat at the central one, whittling the small matchsticks. Small slivers of ebony lay at his side. A piece of tree trunk stood up in front of him like a chopping block. The women brought out gourds of liquor and left them at the fires and the men all came out to drink. They brought with them the huito fruit, which they pounded and put into the embers. The boys crawled out of the hut and lined up in front of Yoreitone. These were the boys who had sat and listened to him the other day, the day I heard the end of his talk of women. They were as silent now as then. Yoreitone held up his mace and, in a loud voice, began to chant.

"Fill the emptiness!"

A man of thirty or thirty-five came up and took hold of the shoulders of the first boy and pushed his head down to the edge of the tree trunk. Yoreitone, still chanting, put a sliver of ebony into the coals of the fire, twirling it there with both hands for some seconds, then pulled out the lower lip of the boy so that it rested firmly on the flat of the trunk and pushed the sliver through the flesh, removed it immediately and shoved a small match-like stick into the hole. "Fill the emptiness!"

No cry was heard as the ebony pierced the lip and the boy got up, blinking his eyes and smiling happily. The man, his father, led him to one of the fires and scrubbed his body clean with a bundle of fibers and thistles. He had looked before as if he had come out from a black bath of ink and now his flesh was a shining light brown, all ready for the new designs, like those on myself, Michii, and Darinimbiak, that were being patiently painted upon him, beginning with the inverted vees on his breast.

The whole of the day went by before the last line of paint had been drawn on the body of the last boy. No one had gone inside the hut, except for the women who brought out the liquor, which we each drank down, bowlful after bowlful. Laughter began with nightfall and from the blackness we crawled into the smoky light of the hut. Some women were in all of our small partitions, others remained around the fires and the newly made men, as well as the others, went up to them without a word, embraced and began to couple. Michii lay down on top of the woman with whom he had fathered a child. We others found arms stretched up in welcome. Strange, inevitable, holy, to feel that soft flesh beneath my hands and body. Sleepless hours passed and I got up and went outside and in my mind took a piece of orange paper and with a pair of scissors cut a small circle, pasted it on a sheet of ultramarine light, cut from black the shape of treetops and stuck them inches below the moon, held out the collage and saw the sky.

13

Is it to you, M, or to you C, that I wish to address this? Are you now all become one, my friends and diary, so that I can barely distinguish you one from the other? Or is it only the terror or horror that came over me that day of murder that binds together your world into one, having faded into the mist of my memory and you float there at this moment of writing with but a single mind, and I lie here ready to cry out and scream my innocence to you, to myself, to Michii, Manolo, Darinimbiak, to every leaf and animal, to every sky and every moon, to every cloud and drop of rain, to every day and night, to every painting that I've ever painted? What had I released from inside me that day I first set foot inside a jungle and I could not see the violence of those strangling vines, of plant life fighting for a bit of sun, nor insects sending forth venom? Instead perhaps a dybbuk entered me, the spirit waiting for the day I crossed a threshhold of unknown self, lying dormant all these years in patience until a time it knew would come, the time perhaps when I prepared myself with practice every morning with my friends, to shoot my bow and arrows till I felled a flying toucan, two wild turkeys, and another bird they called a mee-ekana, with orange breast and wide black wings. For years I had practiced on a violin, making music heard by none but me; for weeks I practiced with a different bow and those birds that I impaled were sources for a hundred joys that covered me with gooseflesh and sent sensations through my groin.

There came another hunting trip with many men, and me among them freshly painted, going farther and farther into the forest, carrying in my hand my bow and arrows, while they carried theirs, too, and axes of stone as well. The rains of the season had already begun and sheets of water drenched the jungle and flooded the rivers. Streams turned into raging torrents, and we would cross them slowly, leaning against the current, the water rushing violently over our legs; quickly it reached our waists and we strained to make headway, holding our weapons above our heads. Michii grabbed my hand and ran at an angle with the current until there was no bottom and we were suddenly being swept downstream and finally jolted into a far bank. Thick mud was everywhere and we sank deep into marshes and struggled in slime, pulling ourselves out by grasping vines. It was any day and any time of my life, the rain a little heavier. The scarlet of our faces was streaked with water and dropped in stains that paled upon our bodies. A silence came over the whole of us and we stood in a small open area on wet leaves and formed a circle around our propped-up arrows and axes, our arms on each other's shoulders, so close our hips were touching, and we swayed back and forth, heads leaning to one side. "Ooooo-ooooo," we whispered in a low growl. "Ooooo-ooooo," the sound came out from deep inside, sending a shiver along the line of arms. Michii broke from the circle and stepped inside, the gap closing in a smack of flesh. He held up his penis and began to rub it hard. He walked to the man beside me who was himself then half erect, and touched the ends of their penises together, then moved in a counter-clockwise fashion from one to another, pressing slightly on each penis with his own, ending up with mine, and re-entering the circle at my side. We growled once again in whispers and I wondered at this ceremony, performed so far from home, thinking not where it might end or why no one had shot the nutria we had startled in its sleep, but only thinking in the present and allowing all to enter in.

The rain had stopped, the sun had long gone down, no moon had risen. Small animals rustled on leaves, a monkey howled, a bird shrieked. We walked noiselessly. The smell of smoke drifted toward us and I heard the muffled sounds of a village, not our own. My companions, twenty-three of them, went on in single file, and then broke into groups as the forest opened into a clearing, each group moving toward one of the several huts. Michii took me by the elbow and pulled me along with Darinimbiak and Ihuene, Baaldore and Reindude, all those among whom I spent each night. Great cries of EEEEE-eeeee!! hit the air and ears as we ran into a fire-lit hut and animal arrows in front of my eyes were used as spears, and axes split into skulls. I stood and watched, no word or sound from me, but shaking, trembling with cold, my breathing coming in gasps. No time was passing, but seven men lay there dead, bellies and chests open, still pouring out hot blood, heads crushed and dripping brain, while women huddled far in a corner, chanting in deep moans and holding the fright-filled faces of their children into the red paint of their breasts. The bowels of the men had opened and their feces oozed out and mixed with their blood. They stared at me, the dead, their eyes wide or half opened, one with a line of white running from his mouth crossing over the black triangles painted on his face, another with a hand resting in the fire and his back curving over a log, a pair of them wound together as if about to begin an act of love and held one upon the other with a single spear. The others were strewn around and lay like dummies carelessly dropped, except that skin was torn and cut and dark red bubbled up from holes. The living laughed and threw their arms around me, and Michii took an arrow from my hand and plunged it through an inert breast. With another arrow he sliced through the string that held a penis stiff against an abdomen, and the penis curled and slipped between its thighs. Outside, my stomach turned upside down, but I went on with them to look in other huts, where other dead lay in other positions, and against the background of the unending moaning of the women, the crying of the children, was the laughter of my people. Not one had a scratch on him, it was over so quickly, and once, even, I laughed with them.

One body from each hut was brought out and dismembered. The heads were cut off and tossed by the hair to the edge of the compound. All viscera was removed, cleaned, and wrapped in leaves and placed with its body. The torso and limbs were tied to poles. A few of what seemed to be the healthiest women and children, those that weighed the most, were rounded up, none protesting and no longer moaning, and we all set out for home, in a long, chattering, lively procession.

We did not sleep that night, but walked on until the early morning, when we reached our river, where we washed, and then we rested. In the light of day, in the thoughts that ran through me, I could not sleep, but rested my head on Michii's chest, with Darinimbiak's legs woven with mine. It was evening, and I had dozed at times before I felt Michii move out from under me and we three got up and crossed with all the others to where fires were burning in the open and human flesh was already roasting, not tended by women now, but by the younger boys who had not come with us. Yoreitone held out his feathered mace. He circled each fire and grunted out words that soon became a chant. The men went into the hut and brought out their own maces and decorations, the first I had seen of them, and joined him to form a huge oval that encompassed all the fires, and all began to sing.

Mayaarii-há, mayaarii-há
Eyorii-kihuat
Ihuenuayken
Hinkaá-hinkaá
Ihuenuayken, ihuenuayken
Mayaarii-há, mayaarii-há . . .

It was chanted in low hoarse voices, with long drawn-out syllables in only three notes. The refrain was repeated over and over and the last line had no ending so that the song could go on with no break before the first word began again. They bounced in dance up and down, twice on one foot, twice on the other.

Roaring jaguar, roaring jaguar
Who wanders over the bank of the river Eyori
There you are saying
This is how I growl, this is how I growl
Here I am, here I am
Roaring jaguar, roaring jaguar . . .

They wore headdresses of red and yellow macaw feathers, and rings of long feathers were looped over their shoulders and in movement they spread and waved like wings. They carried the long maces, topped with bunches of short parrot feathers glued together with wild black beeswax and tied on loosely with fibers, ten or twelve bunches to a mace that hit one against the other, as the mace bounced up and down, hard wax cracking against hard wax to the

same movement and rhythm that their necklaces of
bone rattled round their necks, all of it together
making a spectral sound, rustling, clattering. The figures hovered about the fires, black silhouettes, or blaz-
ing copper and gold when the flames' reflection struck
their bodies. They danced without tiring, sometimes
undulating and swaying, the long plumes blurring
from their backs in flight, and when I entered the
circle, I was hypnotized by movement always up and
down, kaleidoscopic lights that flickered through my
iris, a chant that soon became a roar that drained out
thoughts that came my way, and hours later when I
sat with Michii and with Darinimbiak, the three of
us alone at the fire with others dancing, singing
around us, I took a piece of meat that Michii held out
and ate and swallowed and ate some more, and entered
the circle again to dance. Mayaarii-há, mayaarii-há!!

A curve of moon came up and lined a black cloud
with grey. Its light covered us all with blue as we sat
or lay around the fires, eating, moaning the tones of the
chant, swaying forward and back, moving from the
hip, forward and back. Calm and silence settled over
us, all men. Four got up, one picked a heart from the
embers, and they walked into the forest. Small groups
of others rose, selected a piece of meat, and disappeared in other directions. We three were alone until
Ihuene, Baaldore and Reindude were in front of us,
Reindude cupping in his hand the heart from the
being we had carried from so far away, the heart of
he who had lived in the hut we had entered to kill.
We stretched out flat upon the ground, lined up, our

shoulders touching. Michii looked up at the moon and showed it to the heart. He bit into it as if it were an apple, taking a large bite, almost half the heart, and chewed down several times, spit it into a hand, separated the meat into six sections and placed some into the mouths of each of us. We chewed and swallowed. He did the same with the other half of the heart. He turned Darinimbiak onto his stomach, lifted his hips so that he crouched on all fours. Darinimbiak growled, Mayaarii-há! Michii growled, Mayaarii-há!, bent down to lay himself upon Darinimbiak's back and entered him.

It is written down on paper now and there's no turning back, no erasing, no washing out the brain with turpentine, no telling myself it was all a dream. I can read it here myself. In Singapore, I met a man, a doctor married to a heathen Chinee, a beautiful, brilliant woman who bore him equally beautiful, brilliant children. He himself was British, with a Russian name, and he had been sent the year before by the British authorities to make a study of the Murut people, who lived in the center of what was then called North Borneo. He was a medical doctor and went there as such, to find out why the tribe was dying out. He lived some months with them and came away with no certain knowledge, but only a theory that met with derisive laughter. The Muruts had been headhunters, and when I myself went on to stay with them, there were still heads hanging from beams and set on shelves under eaves. They had been a fertile tribe, babies plopping out of wombs each year to grow up healthy and strong, with nothing more than outbreaks of malaria to keep them from over-running the island. The war came and the Japanese offered other types of heads, their own, for them to slice and hang. When the British returned and took control, the cutting off of heads was stopped and then, according to my doctor, then, the tribe began to waste away. He had no evidence but the year of sterility's beginnings, the talks with elders of the kampongs, and examinations that might have showed a weakening of muscles but no lack of strength in other areas of the body. No evidence, but somehow, coincidental with the British law, a lack of children being born.

"It could not have been clearer," he said to me, "but they laughed as if I'd told a joke."

14

Darinimbiak has been ill for the past two days with diarrhea. I had brought along inside my knapsack, as I always do wherever I go and luckily have never had to use for myself, a tube of enterovioform tablets, and the six I've already given to him have had no effect. It doesn't seem serious, but it has been disturbing him to get up at night, and once he got no further than a few feet from us before he had to squat and empty himself, groaning with pain. It hurts to hear his groans, but others laugh and he laughs too.

Here I'd been so closed inside my own contentment that it occurs to me only now that in all my time living my time, there have been no deaths within our hut. I have never counted heads, which I might have done during my first days, and was never aware of any disappearances that could have taken place before I came to know each face so well. There were two pregnant women whom I noticed one day with flatter bellies and no babies on their backs, but there was no sign of grief, no service of which I was a part. No older man has fallen in his tracks, grasping at a convulsing heart, no hunter has returned all shredded from the claws and teeth of a jaguar, no fever has yet kept anyone bedded down. Awaipe has sores creeping along his back and side as if he'd somehow contacted syphilis, and young Pendiari has a lump on the back of his head that seems a little larger every day, but neither one complains, and they are sources more for curiosity than embarrassment or disgust. Even if I had the medicines of Manolo's pharmacy with me, I wouldn't know what to do with them. It is strange now to be thinking of illnesses and death again. No, not so strange.

I am a cannibal.

That four-word sentence doesn't leave my head. No matter into what far corner of my mind I push those words, they flash along the surface of my brain like news along the track that runs around the building at Times Square. So thoughts of death are natural now as love, I tell myself, and I repeat it on and on, hoping some impression will be made. It is a simple truth of this life, and Michii and Darinimbiak can live in no other way that would keep them as they are, the way in which I continue and will forever love them. What monster do I become that I can write and think so cruel a combination of words! Better let me lie sleepless again another night like last, when I chanted to myself Shema, Hear, Ysroel, O Israel, Adonoi, The Lord, Elohenu, our God, Adonoi, The Lord, Echod, is One. There was a certain element of comfort thinking out excuses for those killings, but none would hold in any way, and I cannot help but judge myself even in the role of onlooker, helpless for a moment, yes, helpless to react, but later surely taking part. In that past life of mine in which I could not live the norm and take an ordinary job, marry and have children, I set myself apart, seeing no pleasure in the marriage covenant, or in a TV set or bridge or in owning any kind of car. And then I came out here and for the first time joined a real community, immersing myself within their lives as best I could, not deeply enough I see now to go deeper into their whole way, to become an honest one of them, not thinking back to that other day on which I wrote I'd always necessarily have knowledge they could never know or feel, but going even where I never thought to travel into inner consciousness and asking my flesh and blood to turn my centuries back to their beginnings. This is a limitation of my own, not theirs, and if I sit in judgment on myself, it must remain only me whom I judge, for I have come here into a new world, from a world as strange in other ways, a world which always troubled me.

How long have I been here? Ten weeks? twelve? M! are you listening? How far would you go to rid yourself of your arthritic pains? What sun would you inhabit for the heat that would relieve you? Ten weeks of cure before the aching starts again is long enough for almost any settlement, and my painful days begin to dim away when I resort to medicines of loving arms, of arrows striking birds, of moons that fill the sky, of heat that draws the senses into misting waves. Manolo! are you too listening, laughing up your buttonless sleeve?

M once said to a friend, "The only way to write a book is to sit down at the typewriter and write." The only way I find to empty, to exorcise, to refill myself, is to write across these pages, but something now has happened to that urgency that had compelled me almost daily to pour onto paper the words that flowed like liquid from my hand. Today, I sit a minute, an hour, to add two words together, fearful of the phrase they make and it has taken me almost the whole of the day to put down what is here. I can go no further, thinking to explain, because the explanations are perhaps for C and M. It may be that I don't need them.

15

Last night I couldn't sleep at all. Darinimbiak was up and down at least ten times and all my enterovioform is gone. We will go to the mission to see if Manolo can be of help. Darinimbiak is losing weight and his color is a little grey. Michii wants to come with us and the others of our sleeping compartment, and I thought it would be a good idea to take along Awaipe and Pendiari and see what can be done for them. Michii and I talked with Yoreitone this morning and he made no objections, just grunting. All through this morning we were brought presents to take with us. I've counted up six baby howler monkeys, three parrots, a jaguar just a few weeks old, three lovely birds a deep blue in color, two pink owls (one has a crushed-in head and doesn't look as if it will live very long), and then yuca, pineapples, fish and meat stored in sections of bamboo, and three carrying bags full of peanuts.

I am afraid to go back, partly for myself, partly for what might happen to my people. We leave tomorrow.

16

Seven months have gone by! Do you hear me!
Seven months, that I had thought were three or four!
Twice as long as had been in my mind. Where did all
that time go? What did I do that it passed so quickly,
and I so unaware of its passing? Yet, there it was on the
wall of the veranda, the calendar, another piece of
paper with marks upon it, one that really counted days
and time, and making no mistakes. Wassen has died.
Manolo is dead, just like that, dead. Father Moiseis is
more peculiar than ever. And Hermano seems to have
lost his bearings. These days he talks to me at length
and no longer follows the padre wherever he goes, and
I have a feeling that he's having sex with Itaqui, or
something close enough to sex to make him change so
completely. It had not occurred to me that life at the
mission would not remain the same as when I left it.
The photograph of it on my brain had not allowed
for even a moment to pass. I had expected all to stop,
to stand in the same positions as when I last saw them
at the edge of the compound waving their goodbyes,
and to continue on with that same waving at my return, and seeing such new faces, such new attitudes,

was like entering into another land, one I'd never seen before. The shock to me of Manolo's death turned the mission into some other place, one that I barely recognized. Dead, the padre told me. Just like that, he said when I asked for him. Dead is all he said, and it was also the only word he'd used for Wassen. Hermano wasn't much more helpful during my first two days.

"There isn't any grave, but he's dead. I know. Manolo is dead."

"But how? What happened?"

"I'll tell you when the padre isn't here. We can talk when he goes to Lima the day after tomorrow. If he goes. He might want to stay, now that you've brought him all these new people."

There had been presents, but no farewell rituals when we left our home on the river Hitapo. No waving arms, no goodbyes, no starting along the trail with us for company for a while. We simply went our way, the eight of us, as if we were going out for a swim, or walk, or on the trail to hunt. It took us seven days of traveling slowly to arrive here at the mission, and it rained continuously for three of them, a light rain, a drizzle, a thunderstorm of huge drops beating against the leaves, and a heavy fog through which the foliage cut as we walked by like knife-edged discs of green and grey that sat upon the mist.

Poor Darinimbiak. I thought we'd never get him here alive, and now with Manolo gone, it might have been better if he had died along the way or better still, inside the hut in which he'd had such happy times, in which he knew so well the textures of all his hands and body came in contact with, all the smells, the faces, sounds, and sights he'd always known. Manolo's out-dated books of medicine have shown me what to do with Awaipe and with Pendiari, but nothing for the dysentery that has come to destroy my friend, a friend who now seems closer to me than any of the others of our compartment. On our first day out, he walked so well I thought him feeling better, but when we stopped to eat and sleep, he wouldn't touch the food I cut in tiny pieces, he only drank the water that growled inside his stomach and came out quickly with a roar. The next morning we built a makeshift stretcher of branches, fibers, leaves, and vines, and we carried him. Several times a day we floated him across the flooding rivers and he often moaned but never let out a cry, though I cried out each time we bumped a rock, each time a branch reached out to scrape his skin, at every movement unforeseen that could have troubled him. His bowels opened with no control and I was thankful for the rivers in which to wash him. The food we'd brought along was hardly what he needed, and once, when Baaldore shot a wild turkey with an arrow, I made us stop a while so I could make a bowl of clay in which to boil a soup, but the bowl would not hold together and cracked apart when filled with water. Sad, angry at my own inability to make something so simple as a clay pot, I fed him masticated meat and yuca, but only twice did he eat it.

Darinimbiak was not in the least bit sad himself, in spite of his weakness, and the trip was not without its joys. The birds and animals we carried clutched themselves around our bodies or screamed out from their baskets and made our lives noisy, as if we men were chattering to each other in a language unknown before but learned in these new sections of the forest. As Darinimbiak lay upon the stretcher, he held in his hands the wounded owl and stroked its head, fed it squashed banana and laughed at every swallow. He also watched the steps we took and always looked in all directions, imprinting on his memory those days of different trees and skies. And so the days went by until we came to the small island in the river from which could be seen the rooftops of the mission. We stopped there to build a fire, touch up our body paint, to eat, to await the arrival of Father Moiseis.

There were some occasional sounds as we sat waiting; the wind rising and moving through the trees, dry leaves scratching against dry leaves, a solitary laugh drifting down the river from the mission, and puste birds were cawing as they flocked into a grove of papaya trees. The padre arrived before the sun had set, his kepi on his head and dressed in his stained cassock. He came in a long canoe that was piled with mounds of yuca and bananas. Water splashed over the sides and we watched the canoe jolting on rocks and being swept along by the current almost into a bank of paca. The canoe was pulled up onto the stones of the beach and Father Moiseis stood for a moment at a distance, though not far away, and stared and yelled, "Señor! Señor!" and I got up from my squat as he opened his arms and we hugged and laughed and tears flooded from his eyes.

"We said you were dead! we knew you were dead, and here you are alive and bringing me new people! Caracho! you have done well! but where are your clothes, eh? you cannot be here naked like that with paint looking like a savage, eh? but you will dress when we are at the mission."

He let me go and looked at my seven companions, not one of whom had moved. Wancho and Alejo had remained at the canoe and I went over to them with arms outstretched, but they seemed frightened of me and there were no welcome hugs and smiles as I had hoped, but looks that filled their minds with all my nakedness and all the paint upon my body. They turned to the canoe and emptied the boat of its food. They took out four bamboo poles that were tied together at one end, spread out the other ends and placed the structure upright like a tepee. They tied branches from pole to pole, about four feet above the ground, and then smaller branches were laid across to make a platform. Equipment for Mass was uncovered and set on top of this altar. Father Moiseis dropped his kepi and put the hood of his cassock over his head and began to read the Mass. All of them, Michii, Darinimbiak, Baaldore, Reindude, Ihuene, Awaipe, and Pendiari, all still motionless, sat and watched. When Mass was over, the padre knelt before the men and kissed each one of them. He kissed them on the lips and they moved back as if repelled. They got up and threw their arms around each other and laughed. The padre pinched and tickled them and spoke in Spanish.

"Just you wait, eh? you wait, eh? you will see the Mass again and I will teach you all the love of God and all his words, caracho! but you come here and I will give you presents and you are my children now like all the others and we will work together in the fields, ai! how smart you are to come!"

How smart we are to come! In starless darkness I lay beneath a crackling lean-to, with Darinimbiak's cheek against my own, our group all tied together with our limbs, a cluster of humanity, remaining safely in that world we bound by tightened arms and legs, while farther down the bank of stones, another world, the padre slept within his sleeping bag, with dreams of bringing God to children, and close to him lay Wancho and Alejo curled as one, their machetes almost in their hands. How smart we are to come! I saw how Michii ran his hands along the wood of the canoe, seeing in his eyes the day he would make one for himself. I saw Ihuene watch Alejo slice a branch with his machete, but would not yet go close to hold it. And I heard the padre talk about his Christ and saw another day when all would kneel and eat a human not of flesh, but one of flour that could never fill their stomachs or put muscle on their bones.

How smart, Manolo, how smart you were to go!

Where will you wander now? You have emptied out the mission of my inner food, taking with you all I felt before, and no breath from your lungs remains, nor is there on your bed of bark the slightest sign that it was yours. Where are your papers, eh? all those things you wrote and said some day I would have to read? Did you take them with you, or are they burned or hidden in some recess that I myself will soon discover? Your books are gone as well, except those medical ones you left inside the pharmacy, which taught me how to cut into the lump on Pendiari's head and squeeze out all that pus. Can you see him now with all those white bandages wrapped around his skull, which he pulls off and I put on five times each day? This is all you've left me, now.

In the morning, Father Moiseis got up and came over to us, standing, looking down, frowning his Good morning.

"You will sleep at the mission, eh, señor? and we will wash your paint and give you clothes to wear. Caracho! but it is not good to see a white man this way and then they my children will see that pants are good for them and they will learn how to put them on."

He became irritable as we all entered the canoe, and he scarcely talked at all. My Akaramas felt his coldness but they could not resist the pleasure of the canoe and jumped up and down as soon as the boat was slipped into the water and we tipped and all fell out. Even the padre laughed at their excitement. Darinimbiak seemed more excited than anyone else.

He sat, as we all did, in the clutter of the canoe, but leaned way out and put his head down just above the river's surface, and stared into the water, twice took up his fishing spear but missed each time he jabbed at creatures swimming there.

The beach of the mission was lined with all its inhabitants, including barking dogs. Father Moiseis was the first out of the canoe. He turned toward us, as if he too had stood there waiting, bowed down and spread his arms in welcome. I stepped out, pulling Michii by the hand, then pulled at Darinimbiak, who now seemed full of energy. The others followed after us and the Indians on the bank moved back in fear and went behind the trees and walls and watched us from between their fingers. The Akaramas stopped at the bank of the compound, afraid of the dogs, who continued to bark and snarl until Hermano drove them back. Hermano then came up to me and shook me by the hand and there was more welcome in his saddened eyes then I had ever seen before. The dogs were tied up in the Pueranga huts, and my friends began to look around and entered every open door. They took out utensils from the kitchen, while Santusa turned her face to the wall, and began to bang spoons and forks against the pots, and pans against the stones, and ran along waving shirts and trousers and the padre's long underwear. They found knives and tied them over their shoulders with string, and were about to break some chairs for firewood when Hermano rushed headlong into them and threw the chairs into the diningroom and locked the door. The dogs came out again and Michii hid behind me and kicked out at one. Darinimbiak, now tired and weak, was walking slowly through it all, examining the metal of the knives and pots and showing them to the others, who tried to break them. He held up a knife and watched it shine in the sun, stabbed a piece of wood, pulled it out and brought it over to me.

"From what river does this clay come?" I explained as carefully as I could that it wasn't clay, but another kind of material that came from far over the mountains. Later, I saw him digging at the water's edge, shaking his head. Still later, he was digging beneath the largest hut, directly under the room in which the padre slept. For two afternoons he dug in various spots and always frowned his disappointment.

The dinner bell rang and everyone jumped at the noise and looked around to find what made it. When I showed the bell, they laughed and hit it with their hands, producing a duller sound. They took small rocks and beat the bell until they tired. I ate with the padre and Hermano inside the diningroom, and offered fried meats to Baaldore who squatted next to me and laughed to see us eat with odd utensils. He smelled the meat and shook his head. I gave him salt to taste, a lick of his tongue on my hand, but he spit it out. I tried sugar with the same reaction. Tea and bread brought forth the same disgust. Ihuene and Reindude came in carrying two monkeys for the padre, and I gave all four some bread to eat and they all gave a chew and spat it out. The monkeys, however, lapped at the sugar and stuck their hands in the bowl for more, and cried out when the padre picked it up and handed it into the kitchen to Santusa, who had two parrots on her shoulder.

Michii arrived at the door, chewing on a magazine. I opened it and showed the photographs, but he and the others shook their heads when I said they were people or landscapes, and with no past from which to draw on, they could not connect these images with living beings, trees or hills.

On the veranda, I told Darinimbiak to lie and rest in the hammock in which I had often rested, and had glanced through books and magazines. I brought up some soup in a gourd bowl, and he drank it slowly after first refusing, shaking his head until I told him it was medicine. I put a record on the victrola and wound it up. A voice and music screeched, startling Darinimbiak. One by one, all the others braved the steps that led up to the porch, but stood off in a corner, watching the disc turn around and around. Hermano came up and sat on a chair and beat time to a huayno and changed records. Suspiciously, they approached the box, leaned over it slowly, almost afraid of it, looked around to the other side, under the table on which it sat. I picked up the arm and the music stopped abruptly. They jumped back. I put the arm back down in place and they huddled around me and looked up and down, searching for the tiny people who made this noise, and finally decided they must be inside the box. Ihuene picked up a record from the floor and put it to his ear, was disappointed that it made no sound. He gave the record to Hermano, who changed a huayno for Caruso singing from *Bohème*.

After a while, I found myself also looking for the tiny being who lived inside and sang that scratching tune. We sat and listened to the records the whole of the afternoon, with Hermano clapping hands and stamping the floor to the music's rhythm. Then he wearied and went down the steps. The victrola wound itself down and I took the last record off, saying, "That's all for now." They clapped for more and would have listened through the night, and I did play another and finally thought to say, "The little people are tired now and they must eat and go to sleep."

"Aaaaa-aaaaa, ooooo-ooooo," they whispered. "Yes, they must go to sleep."

Santusa and Hermano had put together some fresh meat and given it to the men, who sat at a fire they made on the beach, and cooked their food the way they knew it. After dinner, attracted by the light and people in the chapel, they went in and sat on the floor. Nude, painted in black and red, they all but melted in the candlelight into the wood and vines that formed the walls and floor. They laughed during the service and sat on the platform, got up and walked around touching everything in sight, and pulled at the padre's vestments. Soon it somehow came to them that this was a place of gods and they sat a while in silence, not moving, watching the gestures of the padre and of Hermano, staring up at a newly acquired, already worm-eaten and molding painting of the Madonna, above the altar.

The padre has been doing no work, refusing to go to Lima, and has been spending his days preparing for and saying the Mass, talking with the men and trying to convert Darinimbiak. Every afternoon he goes off to his room to read his Bible and to nap, and always one or two of my men follow him. As always, he reads, as always, he sleeps, only now they crouch by his bed.

"Well? how do you like my children?" he asked me several times at meals. "Aren't they children?" He took the head of Reindude in his hands and squeezed in the cheeks, patted the face, hugged it to his breast, offered a taste of tapir, not accepted. "A picture, no? are you painting it all? you have them listening to the records? That's a painting, bending over listening to the victrola, you say they come from Hitapo? Maybe you will find some rich American who will send us money for the mission, or a beautiful picture it would make with a woman feeding a baby at one breast and a monkey at another, no?"

Often at the table, I felt that I had never left the mission and that the conversation between myself and Father Moiseis was continuing on from where he had left off so many months ago.

"You will make many paintings of my children and you will sell them and make much money, no? You know there was an expedition that came here and wanted to visit the Indians just like these but they wouldn't listen to me when I told them they shouldn't go first, that I should go first, that they should wait until I talked with them, but you know how people are, always wanting to show off and be the first and my Indians! Caracho! They shot their arrows and there was much trouble but there was a very nice Canadian who came with them who had been in Spain, I liked him, he knew all about my country, but he was just like the rest of them, eh? and what do you think of my children now? It is so nice to have them finally right here and we will talk and talk of God and Christ and they will come to know it all, eh? but that boy he must be the first, he must know God and confess his sins, like you señor have surely sinned living there with them for so long a time, where instead I should have been, I should have brought them to the mission myself, caracho! it is not right that you spent so much time there—you should have come right back, right away, and showed me their village and I would have gone with clothing and machetes and all of them now would be blessed."

17

At this moment in time and space, there is not enough peace or ease or calm inside of me to think out anything clearly and my thoughts just shift around from one to another and I cannot complete a single one of them. You, M, you lie there on your bed each morning for an hour before your breakfast is brought in to you, arranging in your mind the day's work on your novel, while you push aside with pain, all pain. You lie there and think out whole paragraphs and pages long before your secretary arrives to type it up. Yet here I am so confused, disoriented, engorged, by so much happening simultaneously that's beyond my control, that I want to run away again, I want to run back, to run forward, I don't know which, to my home, and take with me all my men, and throw off forever these clothes that rub and irritate my skin, clothes that I'm forced to wear. But really, they are no more than a slight burden that I know so well I must accept and must ignore, instead of trying to turn it all into some kind of symbol. And how? how can I write of so small an irritation when there's so much to discuss that must be clarified and decided upon, to help me once more rid myself of contact with a world I thought I'd left beyond the chain of mountains, but remains, here, there, always within me and which is never gone but for moments, hours, no matter how I try to fool myself.

First, though, I want to talk of Darinimbiak because he's on my mind today more even than Manolo, whose story I heard two days earlier. That he was ill, you already know, and know it well, I hope, for to try to cure him was the main, the only reason for returning to the mission. At our arrival, I thought to put both Darinimbiak and myself in the room in which I had previously slept, but Father Moiseis insisted that he could not sleep there, that it would set a precedent of having a native in the building in which he himself slept, and he preferred to have only white people there. At any rate, the smell of dysentery would overpower and disgust him so that he would not be able to get a good night's sleep. We made our little home, therefore, Darinimbiak and I alone, in a tiny empty hut that had no walls, but only a side leaning its top against another side, a triangle of thatch, open at both ends. I spread two blankets on the bare earth, tied up mosquito netting, and found some other blankets to cover us, for it was cooler here with no fires close by to warm us. I kept two gourd bowls by his side, within easy reach of his hand, and for the first two or three days, he was able to empty himself into them with no help from me. I gave him other pills and injections of penicillin, but they were of no use and had no effect whatever. When he could no longer lift himself upon the bowl, I set it under him myself and there were times when I was out and came back to find the blanket flowing with his feces. I told the padre then that I thought he couldn't live much longer, that none of the medicines with which I treated him were of any help, unless he himself had something that I had not tried.

Each morning I washed Darinimbiak, and I washed him each time he opened his bowels. I had to remove the blanket from beneath him and I replaced it with soft grasses and leaves. He opened his eyes and smiled each time I touched him, but otherwise his eyes were closed and he looked asleep. I would pick up his head and place it in my lap and feed him soup. He was seventeen or eighteen, this friend of mine, but those deep brown trusting eyes gave him the appearance of someone younger. His naked body was always wet with perspiration, which I wiped away whenever I entered. The fringe of hair clung damply to his forehead and the longer strands were pasted against his shoulders. I slept next to him at night and he hugged me close. The odor of feces emanated from the skins of us both and during the day everyone but the padre and Hermano stayed as far from me as possible, though I went often each day into the river, and no one but Father Moiseis and myself ever went into the hut. Not Michii, or Baaldore or Ihuene or Reindude, seemed to have him on their minds. It was as if he were not there among us or as if he had already gone to some other forest.

Late in the afternoon, as the colors outside changed

with the setting sun, the hut grew dark and I would light the candle that Darinimbiak liked to have beside him until I lay down close by to sleep. It was then that the padre came with his Bible in his hand and would sit on a chair above him and Darinimbiak would begin to moan his pain as soon as his shadow fell across him. The padre would talk slowly at first, in a hushed, whispered voice, imitating the Akaramas' manner of speech. The language of the Puerangas, of which he knew a great number of words, was close enough to that of my people so that there was no difficulty in the understanding of sentences, though sometimes individual words were a problem. Father Moiseis intoned and waved his arms and rocked back and forth.

"Ah but you are a poor poor child, so young to leave this world, so young, yes, but with so many sins committed, poor poor child, so many sins, but no more sins will you commit, for you will go to where there is no sin, you poor poor child, you have fornicated and you have killed, these are your sins and others, they are bad things you have done, you poor child with so many sins and awful things on your conscience, but you will go to a place with God with Christ where there is no sin, you have done the worst that can be done on this earth and you must repent of these sins, you will repent, you have sinned and you will confess these sins, all your ways are known to Christ, He has seen your fornications, the terrible things you have done and He says to me that you must confess, He cries down to me from the cross that you must confess, you sinful child, you child so young and full of sin, He has seen it all and waits for you every day, waits for your repentance."

Out of the field of candlelight, I sat close under the thatch of the hut and watched the troubled eyes of Darinimbiak, who had no understanding of what was being said, for he had no sense of meaning for such thoughts as Christ or cross, repentance or sin. How can you teach a human the concept of sin? The longer the padre talked, the faster his words came out, the louder his voice, the more irritable his tone, until he was no longer trying to speak in any style but his own, so caught up was he in his self and his purpose in life.

"But you have sinned and you must pay for these sins in the sight of God if you do not confess, you have lain with many women, you have played with your own sex and have spilled your seed upon the earth, and you have lain with other men I know, these are grievous sins, you are so young I can only thank God he will soon have you in his arms so you will not continue in these shameful ways, you must confess now, it is good you are so young and have not had so many years as others who have confessed to me, but you do not know what it is to burn throughout all eternity, you do not know what it is for your flesh to char with heat, for this is what will happen if you do not confess, throughout all eternity you will burn like a turkey over a fire, day after day, week after week, month after month, year after year, century after century, when the moon moves across the sky and then a smaller moon takes its place and then there is no moon and another moon does come, and again it comes all full and again again, you will be burning all this time, and when the sun travels under the ground and it too walks across the sky and goes down again so many many times you will always be burning, always burning, while the jaguar comes out a baby from its mother and grows up to kill the tapir, you will still be in the fire, crying out in pain and while the baby of the monkey has a baby and that baby grows up to have its baby, you will be screaming out from the flames in a great and terrible pain, your flesh all scorched and horrible, so young you are and so full of sin you are, you must confess and you will live with God and know happiness with the beautiful little figure on the cross, and you will live and be happy and all the sins will be cleansed out of you when you confess and say the words that I will tell you."

Father Moiseis repeated his sermon every afternoon, growing more intense with each passing day, determined that Darinimbiak should be the first of the Akaramas to know God, determined that Darinimbiak should not die without his help.

One morning, only four days ago, when we had been here about two weeks, I awoke to find Darinimbiak with his head turned toward me, his eyes open, staring at me. His breathing was heavy and coarse, and there was blood mixed with the feces on his bed of leaves. I hardly knew him, he had grown so thin in so short a time. The belly that was once so full and round, was now concave, and the bones of his rib cage stood out on his chest with dark hollows between each one, so dark that in the half-light of the hut they looked like streaks of paint brushed there to indicate his new station in life and death. The whites of his eyes had yellowed and had sunk deeper into his head, as had his cheeks. He had no recognizable expression on his face, though a faint smile had widened his mouth, which opened now and then. I got up, went out and brought back some soup. I placed his head as gently as I could onto my lap and offered a spoonful of broth, which he sipped down but would not take another. Words came out of his mouth slowly, with long pauses between the phrases.

"In the night, in the blackness, I saw my brother Ikonoo. He was in the light and I below in the darkness, and he walked in the forest calling out my name. He looked down at me from the heights and he was laughing. He had that morning painted his body and his face was shining and red. Ikonoo was carrying on his shoulder a tapir with an arrow sticking out from its breast. It was a big tapir, but Ikonoo carried it on his shoulder. He put out his hand and spoke, 'Come, brother, come! Come with me and you will have all the tapir we both can eat. Come with me, brother.' Then there was blackness again and there was no Ikonoo and I opened my eyes."

Darinimbiak twice whispered out this dream, twice in exactly the same words, twice reliving the dream itself, stopping again and again to see again Ikonoo as he walked along, to hear again the words he spoke. A kind of restfulness spread over his face, relaxing all its muscles. He closed his eyes and slept.

Father Moiseis, a grim look creasing his brows, came with the evening, with his Bible clutched in hand, a warrior. "It is your time, my child, your time I say to choose betwen our heaven, our Christ, our happiness, or the terrifying burnings of hell. Confess! I say to you. There is nothing for you to fear if only you repent and tell of these sins of yours. Then you will become a Christian, a Catholic, and you will live in eternal goodness, eternal peace. Think now of that endless time of burning, caracho! you cannot want that, the endless time of pain, the endless time of your screaming out, no! You child, come! Come into the bosom of Christ and He will teach you all the knowledge of love."

Look! are those flickering tensions on that face a fear, or is it simply weariness? for Darinimbiak is nodding. His whole head is flushed, his eyes are almost blank. He is saying after the padre all those words in Spanish and Latin, one by one he says them, and the padre has called out and sent for Hermano who comes in with all the armament of last rites.

A quick ceremony was performed and Father Moiseis went outside the hut and straightened his bent back and looked up into the sky and cried the tears of joy that meant his fulfillment. Darinimbiak touched no food that night, nor did I eat more than the bowl of broth intended for him. Father Moiseis ate with his usual delight.

When later I crawled between the blankets next to Darinimbiak, he moved his hand to rest on mine, and when I awoke still in full darkness before the sun had begun to light the day, I found Darinimbiak dead, lying on his stomach, an arm across my chest, a foot nudged under my leg.

Michii came that morning with pods of achiote and we washed Darinimbiak from head to toe in its red. The stiffened body seemed uncertain of itself and resisted our movements upon it, so unlike the resilience the living flesh and blood had shown when touched and prodded by these same hands. Reindude, Baaldore, and Ihuene sat down watching us work, and then the padre and Hermano came. We carried the body on our shoulders into the jungle, and crossed on foot the river to the small island where I had first arrived with the Akaramas and where they still slept each night. At the far end of the island, we dug a shallow grave, put Darinimbiak into it, waited while the padre read a service for the dead, and then covered him up with the sand and stones of the beach. I said a bit of prayer to myself, wishing him well, wherever he is. Aloud, Father Moiseis said,

"Well. Well. Now we have another little angel in heaven."

18

Michii was sitting on stones in the center of the beach of the island, spinning a stick in the palms of his hands to make a fire, surrounded by trousers and shirts already torn, two boxes with matches spilled out and broken, a variety of metal pots, pans, and other kitchen utensils including a colander, two chairs and a table, none standing in its proper position, small knives and machetes, blankets, sheets, and mosquito netting and several pairs of sneakers, some new, some with holes in them.

The other Akaramas were now arriving on a raft from the mission but I could not see from that distance who it was that was poling them. It was the first time I had seen any of them on a raft and when it was beached, I saw that they were alone, only Ihuene, Baaldore, Reindude, Awaipe, and Pendiari.

How strange it is to me now to write that line of names and not include Darinimbiak! The rhythm of the list changes, the rhythm of life changes, and he was the one whom perhaps I loved the most, perhaps because I had tended to his needs in his last weeks, or perhaps there was a look in his eye or the curve of a bone that drew me closer to him than to the others. Or is it now, only now that he is gone that my memory remakes my past? It was only hours then after his burial, but the Akaramas went their way as if he'd never existed, never died, never had been so much a part of their every moment. If only I too could exclude all days of pain and love that are now not present. Michii's thoughts are upon the smoke coming up from between the moss and bits of twig on which he spins his stick, and he looks up for only an instant at the arrival of his friends. He blows on the smoke and a flame comes up and he adds small pieces of wood, quickly building up his fire. The others are laughing, carrying more pots and pans, and Baaldore has two small mirrors in his hand. He waves one in front of Michii's face, then takes up his foot and shows Michii its reflection. Michii wiggles his toes and the reflection wiggles its toes. He knocks a knuckle on the glass, puts it into his mouth and tries to bite it, hits it with a stone and the mirror shatters. "Ooooo-ooooo," they all whisper. Michii takes the second mirror from Baaldore and watches his hand move in it, then he stands and holds it under his penis. He spreads his legs apart and places the mirror just beneath his testicles, then closes his legs to hold it there and he throws out his arms and laughs, he tries to walk, but the glass drops onto the stones and breaks.

Just then, another raft arrives, with Hermano and Wancho. "Señor, please, señor, Father Moiseis says to tell you that you must do something about all this stealing. He doesn't mind the raft so much because the Puerangas can make another, but how will he ever get more pots and pans and clothes if they keep taking everything they lay their hands on? He says to tell you that they must some time learn something about private property. It takes so long to get anything from Lima, even when there is enough money to buy the things."

"Well," I said, "we will not be here much longer and I will bring back most of it before we go. Tell him that we couldn't possibly carry all this back to Hitapo even if we wanted to. He need not worry so much."

Later, we did return to the mission with much that had been taken away. We went on the raft, with Baaldore and Reindude poling it upstream as if they had been poling rafts for years. They did not mind taking back so much of what they had taken away. The pots and pans and blankets had been experimented with, played with, and the old one with the hair on his face wished to keep them in his home, where they were used for making medicines.

19

From that very first affectionate look in the eyes of Hermano on the day I returned to the mission, it was obvious that something extraordinary had happened to him. He had become less of a shadow and more of a solid man, still a humpbacked, short creature, but instead of that wariness, suspicion, anger, hate, he had come to radiate a rather pleasant kind of sweetness, not at all unbecoming in insipidness, and there were times when he seemed to stand so tall and straight that his hump might have fallen down from his back simply from being for once in so vertical a position. He came to me one morning while I was in the kitchen waiting for Santusa to heat the breakfast broth for Darinimbiak.

"Señor, the padre insists that he is not going to Lima and I have things to tell you and to give you from Manolo, but he is not supposed to know about it, so we must go somewhere where he will not see us."

"Just let me feed this soup to Darinimbiak and wash him a bit and then we can take the raft to the island where the Akaramas are. They'll be coming here today like every day and we can be alone. It is time I heard the story."

And so an hour later we sat alone together on the island, while Hermano unwrapped a sheet of oilskin from which he took out a pile of manuscripts and a thick, sealed envelope with my name written across it.

"Manolo gave these things to me for you, saying that some day you would come back, but that he himself never would. He asked that you burn everything once you've read it all, unless you want to keep the letter."

We were silent for a while as I ran my fingers over the pages, feeling once again a part of Manolo. "Go on, Hermano. Tell me what you have to say."

"What is there to tell? I'm sure the letter says more than I can know. The padre and I had no idea that he wanted to leave or that he was even thinking about leaving. He was depressed for a long time after you left, for two or three months. All he did was read his books and write what I thought were letters, but he didn't send any along with the padre when he went to Lima, and there is only this one for you. Then one day at dinner he said he was leaving in the morning, and he was a lot more cheerful and when the padre went to bed he took me to his room and gave me these things and said he was going to do what you did and go off to look for some tribe to live with. I don't know how he knew you would come back, we were sure you were dead. And the padre never said a word about his leaving after all these years of Manolo's living here, and hasn't even mentioned his name except when Iliu came to tell what happened, and then when you asked about him."

Hermano suddenly stopped talking and began to cry, great sobs that shook his whole body. He calmed down after a few minutes and blew his nose between his fingers. "Do you know what he told me? He said I was wasting my life away here and that the least I could do was to have sex with one of the women and just because I have this thing on my back is no reason to imagine that no one would go to bed with me. And do you know something? He was right. I confess it to you here and now and you can tell Father Moiseis if you like, which I don't think you'll do, not like I would have done, but it was the first girl I tried to do anything with in all my ten years here at Piqul, in fact all my life, and she let me have herself as if I were anyone at all, and she a married woman at that. Maybe you've seen me around with Itaqui. She's Patiachi's wife, and she made me feel just like a man and I wasn't even embarrassed about my awful body. She just let me do it to her out in the fields, and now I guess I'm in love with her and I don't know what to do.

"Isn't it the craziest thing? Me, who all my life couldn't bear to look at myself in the mirror and was laughed at for years and years. A forty-year-old virgin I was, running around with the padre from one jungle to another and hurting in myself every time I thought I knew that someone else was having sex, in sin or not didn't matter, it's only that they were using their bodies for what God meant them to be used for and I thought all the time that I was helping God when I spied on them and told about it. And what was I but a sexless being like one of those angels who aren't either men or women, androgynous, is that the word that Manolo used? But don't think it was easy for me with Itaqui. I was so scared I thought I'd die, but she is married and it seemed better to choose someone who'd had experience and could teach me, not a virgin like myself. She did teach me and she teaches me now, and do you know? all that paint on her face makes her more beautiful to me now, though before, all I could think was that it was some terrible pagan design, and that it was up to me to help the padre make her into a proper Christian. And me, a Catholic, it didn't bother me at all and it doesn't bother me now that I have been having sex out of wedlock. I don't know why, but I don't feel I'm being sinful."

It was good to hear Hermano talking out of himself. But at that moment it was only about Manolo that I wanted to hear. "But if Manolo went off to live with some tribe, as he said he would, what makes you think he's dead?"

"Oh, he's dead all right. Like I said to you when you first came back, I know he's dead because I heard all about it. Do you remember Wassen? that funny old witch doctor with the feathers in his face who died out of loneliness or something? He just came here one day all alone and later told you and Manolo all about his people and how they were killed in his village? That's exactly the way Iliu arrived, an old man who was out hunting with his two very young wives because he was too old to hunt and the women did the hunting for him. First time I ever heard of such a thing. Big, strong women they were, and all of them had clothes on. The three of them came and asked if they could stay a while, maybe even live here, and of course the padre was very happy about it, but they didn't like it, I don't know why, maybe because they had to work the fields every day or because the padre wouldn't give them any machetes to keep but they had to give them back every night. One day they were gone without having said anything to anyone. Anyway, a day or so after they arrived, Iliu talked about a white man living in his village and there isn't any doubt but that it had to be Manolo, just the right height and wearing a beard and carrying a rifle with him. It couldn't have been anyone else, and he did tell them about the mission and that he had come from here so you have to believe it was him. They had gone out hunting like I said, Iliu and his two women, just like Wassen was out looking for his herbs and medicines, and when they got back, everyone was dead, exactly as in Wassen's story. They didn't have any problem finding Manolo or in recognizing him, or at any rate a part of him, because his head was on a stake standing right in the middle of the village. Iliu thinks somehow the village was raided because of Manolo, because his was the only head staked, the other heads were just lying around. Of course, they'd taken his body away to eat, or at least they didn't see it anywhere. I wanted to go with some of the Puerangas to bury the head, but Father Moiseis said we were too busy and had to work the yuca and the pineapples, and we had to take care of the people here because he would soon go to Lima again, that the ants anyway by now would have eaten away all the flesh.''

In all probability Hermano continued to talk, but I don't know what he said, for I heard and saw nothing after that. And if I write this down as if Hermano were just stating a few emotionless facts, the fault is mine because I find this the only way to put it down on paper. I have tried my best to be like my Akaramas with regard to death, but of course for me it doesn't work. It wasn't until hours later at the mission that I was able to open the letter from Manolo, a letter that I've read so many times now that I almost know it by heart. It is a wonder to me, now that I think back, that none of this had much effect on my care and love for Darinimbiak, who himself was then only two days from death. I had known for more than a week that Manolo was dead, but in that telling of Hermano's I was horrified at the way it had come upon him and I saw myself again on that day when I became a cannibal. It wasn't until after I had read that letter that I began to feel more stable and a little calmer, and a dullness took the place of pain, and now I can almost, almost, think of it as a happy death. No, not happy, but at least an acceptable one.

20

"My dear friend,

"You have been gone from the mission for three months and I find my life here unbearable. You are gone; found, I hope, not lost, in a world that saves you. Our dear Father Moiseis has been insisting that you have been killed by people or by animals, otherwise you would have come back to the mission by now, but though I say nothing, I know that you have discovered a life where you are and that you will some day return to civilization. You thought that you could be content to live your whole life there in the jungle, but you will find, as I did, that it isn't possible, that there will be other needs for you, needs that cannot be fulfilled in your forest. You will manage it for a year, two years, maybe four, but you will go back to where you came from and will paint your paintings from all that you have learned in your time here, and with that learning in your soul, you will have no other way to live but in a better way than you lived there before, and I hope that it will be enough to sustain you for all of your life.

"It is possible that you will never receive this letter,

that Father Moiseis will die and Hermano would then abandon the mission and go back to his mountains, or that you yourself are dead. Nevertheless I write it, feeling almost secure that you will read it.

"Your presence here for so short a time forced me again into thinking about myself. There was nothing specific that you said or did that brought about this thinking, not even that you went off in such an astonishing way, but that you were covered when you first arrived, with the veneer of a world that brought back too many memories that made me search out some meaning to my own presence, my own existence, here or anywhere else, the why of why I myself was put onto the earth, a question that so many others have sought the answer to. I have loved so deeply that the aching of my heart and of my soul could not be ministered to by anyone, not even by a loving partner. I nail myself onto the cross each time I love and I cry out each time, 'O God, O my love, why hast thou forsaken me?' for no matter how I try, no matter what I do, the manner of my love is such that it closes in upon itself and forms a hard shell around it, so that nothing goes out, nothing goes in, and the shell begins to grow inside me, suffocating me, blocking the flow of blood to my brain, which then can barely function, except as an extension of my love. It is something that I know I do to myself; I love and I do not allow love to be returned.

"The world of the mission of course sees me as something else. I appear to be happy enough and I do all my good deeds in the pharmacy and dig up the earth and have my hidden pleasures with the boys. I don't argue with Father Moiseis no matter what I think of what he happens to be doing at the moment. It wouldn't surprise me at all to find out that he says you are dead because he's so jealous of you and where you are, and in his mind you have taken away the delight he should have had in meeting new peoples. He always tells that story of that huge expedition having come and everyone wanting to be the first to have contact with his precious Indians, but it was just as important to him to be first with them again, to show the influence he had because he had been with them before. I'm sure he'd rather think you dead than think you could be living with people he himself has never seen. He is, after all, the great missionary and he should be the first one they accept. His need is to believe that God is protecting him and keeps him safe when he meets savages.

"While I was still up in the mountains, wending my way down to the mission, I met a man who was running for the office of mayor of a small town, and the platform on which he ran was that if elected, he would get rid of all the Indians in the jungle, not saying how he would go about it, so that the civilized people could all come into the forest and build their haciendas and cut down the ebony and mahogany and not have to worry about arrows in their backs. He went on to say that they, the purer Spanish, should long ago have done in Peru what the North Americans did in the States, which was to kill off all the Indians and thus avoid having any further difficulties with them. Father Moiseis had a plan to get the government to allot him a great section of the jungle that would be a reservation, and no strangers but scientists could enter it. He told me about this the first day I got here, after I had mentioned this man I'd met, and I thought how wonderful the idea was, and how wonderful is this padre. But it was only an idea about which he soon forgot and he never spoke of it again here or on his trips to visit the head of the mission in Lima. I might have pushed him into it, but after being here some weeks, I saw how his plan would work, with him as the director of the reservation, traveling around with his Bible in his hand, from one village to the next, preaching godliness and shame and desire for money to buy more clothes, more machetes, more victrolas, stopping all the drinking, all the sex out of wedlock, and changing them in much the same way they would be changed by any civilization that came close to them.

"But all that is neither here nor there and no longer has anything to do with me. I have lived here for over ten years and could have lived here another ten, going on in this same way, except that you brought with you maybe conscience and I was beginning to see myself from your eyes, or rather as I would see myself had I been looking out at me from your body, and I didn't like what it was I saw. If there isn't much that one can say against me, neither is there much that one can say *for* me. By which I mean, why am I here? and why have I remained here all these years if not out of a stupor from which I must escape. When you left, I thought about your going and why you went and what you were going into, what you thought you were going into, and what you hoped to find there, though you never really said anything about that, only that you were compelled to go. For a month I worried that out, about myself that is and where in the world was my end and what I was serving by staying here. Anyone can tell me of all the good I'm doing with my penicillin and sulfa drugs, but more basically, I see that I'm not doing anything either for these Indians or for myself and I've come to the conclusion that I am more important to myself than they are to me, than anyone is, and you can call it any kind of selfishness you like, though you won't because I know you understand what I hope I'm saying. The thing is that I've always wanted myself to be really useful in some way, and frankly I'd have liked it to be in a loving, sensual way, almost in the way that the body of Christ is used in communion, and filling souls with love. I want, for a change, instead of someone else filling me with love, for me to fill someone completely, even if it literally means that my flesh and blood must enter into another body. It isn't easy for me to say this to you because it isn't easy to think it out to the conclusion I'm looking for. I have myself, and I have an end, but it's the road to that end that's giving me trouble. I've had dreams of my body being eaten by men and it thrilled me in such an indescribable way that I had an orgasm before I realized what was going on inside of me. I wonder if such a dream or thought ever passed your way? No, it would be impossible. It would be far too revolting.

"Have I ever told you that I love you? Never of course did I say it in any words, but have you never felt it, have you never seen it in me? Maybe I'd love any man who came in this direction, but you came with such an extraordinary simplicity that at first I had to laugh, you with your dreams that had been my dreams, the same dreams that I had thought to fulfill here and instead, have been nothing but a failure, and then here you come thinking as I had thought and what could I do but laugh to myself, and then cry to myself because suddenly it did seem possible in you that here was one person who might well work at finding one of life's solutions, and maybe you wouldn't find much, but you would find something because before you left the mission you had already found more than I had found in ten years, and I know that by the time you read this, you will have found at least a touch more of that solution. How many people on this earth have found even that much? But what my own failure is, I think, is that I have never allowed life to enter into me, that for years I went out in search of it and thought about it and thought about it, and looked for more years even in monasteries, hoping that God Himself was a solution, but it never was for me, perhaps because again I thought too much and simply because there are men like Father Moiseis who turn out to be stupid in my eyes is no reason to think that all men are stupid. I know very well that there are human beings and priests among them who do good with their selfishness, and they do help helpless people to come to some sort of dignity. What I want cannot be told in words, but is only to be felt, or what is more likely is that it's not clear enough in my mind for me to express it. It is something that I knew was in you and there was a time when I thought we could manage a life together, but I was never able to word it out, to put it into sentences, in any way, but what I hoped was that a look on my face, which you never saw, would explain it all. You saw so much here, so much more than I saw when I first arrived, but you didn't see me except as a friend and I wanted more than that and I thought that you were capable of giving it. I wanted *you*; I wanted you in possession, ownership, I wanted you to give yourself to me in a way, to such an extent, that I could even go so far as to eat you while you watched me do it. I think of the love I have to give to the world. I think of myself exploding the energy of love, of that shell inside me bursting apart and sending shrapnel bits not to cut and harm the flesh, but to enter into it and invade the bloodstream with all the gentleness I can offer, sending through each nerve a piece of compassion that would rest the body and soul and allow me, me, myself, to be acceptable before Thee O Lord, my God. But you went off and left me again alone surrounded by people, my problem, people for whom I have no understanding, wanting to be accepted, but accepting nothing, wanting to be loved but only loving myself, wanting a world that never permitted me to exist because I never permitted that world to exist as it was, but only as I wanted it to be, and how could anything be but what it is and no one's thinking will ever change it. If I want to accept you, believe in you, I must accept what you are, not what I want you to be, not what you might have been in my mind. Think how much the same we are, think how different! You will always be discovering new lands, maybe only on your canvases, whereas I have finished my wanderings, and Father Moiseis can forever remain Father Moiseis, for I know that nothing I can think or do will alter his soul or his presence in the slightest. If you live each moment to its fullest, you are living, but once you begin to think Oh! now I am living! you are lost. Lost.

"For I am surely lost now. And I see no living or dying but that they are the same thing. If I am dead inside me, what is life to me? I have no theories about an afterlife, and at this very instant I believe that there can be none, that death is nothing more than extinction, oblivion, an absolute end to all, but in this same instant, I am lost and there is nowhere to go, no one on whom to make my mark, no one who will some day say Where do you suppose he is now, or What a pity Manolo isn't around to enjoy this moment, or If only I could reach out and touch him now. I don't ask for much. I don't think that I ever have. What I ask is only to love in peace, and that has never come to me and of course never will, and so I must somehow bring to a close an existence that has never been anything but excessively painful. I'm not sorry that I'm writing all this down for you to read. Maybe it's that I need to torture someone else for a change, tired as I am of torturing myself, and you are the most likely person. But there isn't much choice, is there? If I write at all, it must be written to you, because I love you, because you are the only one who might know what it is I'm talking about, because you are certainly the only one who could ever be more than someone I listen to, more than someone whose words do more than just go in my ears. I well remember that day I told you of my episodes with my Puerangas who followed me into the fields, and how barren the experiences had become, but that the experiences had given me life. For a whole month, soon after your departure, I knew no one but myself, a project that I planned to see how I would feel, and it turned out to be just as pleasurable because my mind was able to throw its thoughts as arms around a someone else, and that someone else returned the embrace. Yet, after the month passed, I went back to the fields, because my bed became so empty, so lonely, and there was no reason I could think of that made any difference between my own and another's body, though I don't even know for sure why it was that I wanted to make that experiment.

"Where have I led myself in this letter? Surely there's something missing, something I meant to say but haven't even begun to think about, yet I am finished. Maybe all these pages are to tell you that I cannot find any reason to live any longer. The emptiness of death cannot be more painful than the emptiness of life. I too am jealous of you, because you are doing what I wanted to do, what I expected to do which I never until now have had the courage to attempt. To go off into the completely unknown. My jealousy has given me the courage and I will be gone long before you return. The miseries I've evolved within myself are already of the past and I begin for once to evolve a sense of contentment. Let us now pray. Missionary that I was, let me missionize myself from madness to sanity.

"An afternote: I am leaving this letter for you along with all my manuscripts in the hands of Hermano. You can read or not read the manuscripts, as you like, but I want them to be destroyed when you are done. If I live at all, I prefer to live in a friend's memory, rather than on paper. Wish me luck."

21

Well? what do you expect of me now? and what can you tell me of what I was supposed to feel and think when I read that letter? Where was it meant to lead me? You, both of you of whom I think and feel when I write here, you, who have absorbed so silently all these pages, without ever a word of reproach or a word of kindness, of understanding, can't you give me my answer? Manolo writes that I have found something, something that I could take along with me wherever I go. I sensed at once that the letter was written more for me than for himself, that he wanted to tell me of myself, more so even than a telling of why he wished to go into an unknown world, even that he hoped his have left forever? And what on earth *is* that someway I have found something that will carry me through all my days, why does he suggest it will not be here among my people where I remain, but that it will carry me through the days of my return to a land I have left forever? And what on earth *is* that something? Why can I not know of it myself? and why am I always questioning so stupidly, so intensely? Am I so dumb that I cannot figure anything out for myself? I have made for myself my own interior landscape, whether I did it consciously or unconsciously doesn't matter, but that landscape is covered with all this flesh so dense it prevents my looking through it into myself. Seven months I was able to live without this covering, except for a time when we raided a village, seven months of incredible freedom I had not known could exist anywhere, even in a heart. For love is freedom, C once said to me, and I have loved, I've loved and love now, friends, trees, skies, life. And now, what heart is there left to love and mourn Manolo? Hermano's? because of a talk that has given him dignity? My own? because I was loved and because Manolo was able to open himself to me? Manolo must always be a part of Hermano's mind and heart now, and he will always be to him a great and glorious being. Had Manolo not gone away, he could never have been able to talk to Hermano as he did. Nor could he have talked with Hermano had he not written that letter to me and left those manuscripts with him to hold, so the circle begins to open, and who else shall we include as mourner? The dead of Iliu's village perhaps? An Arab in a desert who might still be responding to his touch? If Hermano alone were left to think him great, to remember only that one hour of talk, might it not be enough for a man to have lived? Here I am at the mission, having suffered the pain of Darinimbiak and the pain of his death, a painful suffering death to which I brought him, a death that would have left his mind at ease had he not come with me out of his own time and place. Here I am at the mission, having read a letter about another death, the death of a man who was driven out of his own time and place because his suffering forced him to search for tranquility, for a way not only of life, but also a way of death that might give him peace. Darinimbiak lived out his life without having given thought to happiness, yet he died concerned with sin, evil, hell; Manolo thought about happiness all the time of his life, and it was only at the moment of his death that he might have allowed it to come into him. Or is all this nothing more than an invention of my own to satisfy myself that at least one of these deaths will in some way console me? Am I trying to cancel out what I make into the horror of Darinimbiak's dying by giving into Manolo's dying a sense that was not really there? If only I could know! Let me take these pages one by one and add me up and let me know the sum of myself! But wait! There is yet more to add, there are also the days to come, the years of living with Michii and Yoreitone and Ihuene that will keep me awakened and alive, and all these thoughts will empty themselves from my brain, flow out from each of my openings and leave me free again.

22

Manolo had given his papers to Hermano to hold for me on one day and gone off the next morning, and so it was with Hermano. Having placed this responsibility into my hands one day, he disappeared the next. Father Moiseis read the Mass alone that morning for the first time in over thirty-five years, after which he came into the diningroom without a word and sat to eat his fried bananas. He began to tremble and could not spear the fruit with his fork.

"Where is he? What has happened to him?" Coffee splashed from his cup onto his beard and cassock. "Where could he have gone without telling me? How can there be Mass without him?" Tears came out of his eyes. "So many years together, all of his life together and this is the first time without him." His chair fell backwards onto the floor as he got up, leaving his breakfast unfinished, having managed to swallow only two pieces of banana. He went up to the veranda with his Bible and sat on the hammock. "Señor!" he called down after a moment, "you will let me know when you see him, no?"

Patiachi came into the diningroom, chewing on sugar cane. His long hair had just been cut off that morning and what remained stood out all around his head. He offered me an end of cane and smiled. "They are gone, señor. Gone in the night. Old Heavyback and Itaqui. She was not by me this morning and no one has seen Hermano. It is possible that it is good." He picked up a handful of the fried bananas that had been left by Father Moiseis, and stuffed them all into his mouth, took another handful and went out.

Father Moiseis appeared, at lunch, as if he had washed his face with soap and water, removing the color the sun had given it, and then somehow had also drained out the blood. He was very white. "I knew it, señor! I knew it, that she would take him from me! Caracho! He thought I did not know what was going on, didn't he? But I knew and after all the years together he leaves me like this, with a prostitute, oh, I knew all right, these savages, I give them my life and they treat me like this, I brought him up from a baby as if he were my own child and I taught him how to read, caracho! What more did he want from me—such a good boy he was, always with me, and I never laughed at that evil on his back like everyone else, I heard them laugh, but wasn't I good to him, señor? wasn't I always more powerful than the devil? giving him good and God, and this prostitute comes to take him away, who will help me now with the Mass? I am old, señor, an old man, too old to be left alone with no one to help me, but I knew it when I saw him looking at her months and months ago, when it first began, and all this time it has been going on and now there is no one by me, no one to help me."

Days passed and one evening, only last night it was, I went to the island to spend the night with my Akaramas for the first time since we came to the mission. Baaldore was not there. Michii said he had gone back to Hitapo, and I said that we would all be going in a day or two. The bandage had long been gone from Pendiari's head, and the sores on the back of Awaipe had almost completely cleared up. We slept in a bundle and I felt again at home, my head on naked soft flesh, a head on my own naked soft flesh, my bare back back again on earth. The great piles of pots and pans had long since been returned to the mission and the excitement of all the new things, the toys, except for the machetes, had dwindled to no more than a vague interest, decreasing even further at the thought of carrying them back to the hut. Two pairs of trousers, though, had been split apart, and lay beneath Awaipe, protection for his back. There was a hollow in our bundle and my mind filled it with Darinimbiak, and when in the moonless blackness of deep night I unconsciously stretched out a hand to lay upon a shoulder, it was on his shoulder that it rested. The sound of the river rushing over rocks and gravel awakened me several times and once I saw that Michii's eyes were open, looking into my face.

"You do not sleep?" I asked.

"I do not sleep." A whisper so slight, I had almost to read his lips.

"Do you think about our place in our hut by the river?"

"Yes, I think much about it now."

"We will go together in two days, if you will wait one more day."

"I will wait for you." He closed his eyes then and slept.

At dawn, this morning, our bundle unraveled itself and we ate cold yuca from the ashes of the fire that had gone out during the night. It was a spiritless morning, as if the very air itself had denied its own aliveness, and we all of us moved weighted down by limbs without energy, by limbs with no response. I went alone to the mission and found Father Moiseis in a field with a spade, turning over the earth in which he would plant corn. The color had returned to his face. "So you are back, eh? Let us have Santusa make us some tea." He left the spade planted in the ground and he walked quickly to the compound of the mission, no longer the sad old man.

His appetite had returned and he ate meat and drank three cups of tea. His talk had also returned and the words came out of his mouth as if he could not hold them back, spitting out bits of cracker along with all the words.

"You are going also? Go! eh? Go! You are going back with your savages into your evil, eh? after I teach them about God, you take them away, eh? you and Hermano and Manolo you are all the same, all the same, nothing but evil in this world and it is good that they have gone and that you are going, I have my God with me and He is enough for I will always have Him with me, always He is enough for anyone, let me tell you a story, señor, can I tell it to you? eh? A man came here to the mission one day many years ago, he came on a raft, a raft he said he had built himself and it was a good one, a young man he was and he had a rifle and he brought with him on the raft a big jaguar and some books, a jaguar that he had killed, beautiful is it not? to arrive here with a jaguar? And he had only the torn clothes he was wearing and I gave him new clothes and together he and I and Hermano we built this house in which we all lived because he wanted to stay here with me and help me with my people, and every morning and every evening he came to Mass and he prayed and he made his confession to me, oh! the evil he confessed I could not believe my ears but he became one with Christ and I absolved him of all those sins, do you hear me? I absolved him of those sins, sins that only God can hear and not feel shame, and you too are full of those same sins with your savages, I know, but I absolved him and he was happy and he laughed often, it was good to have him here, caracho! It was good and I went to Lima happy with him remaining here and I came back with medicines that he used for all the illnesses of my people, and I tell you that he was happy here and we all loved him, but one day he was suddenly writing, maybe a year maybe two after he had come, he was writing page after page in a language I could not understand, and why should he write in a language not his own I do not know, and he seemed sick as if he had malaria with trembling, but he had no fever, and then he began to go off into the jungle alone and soon I saw that Wancho or Alejo or someone else followed after him, do not think that I am all blind, señor, I see, I had heard those first confessions of his, I see and I do not say anything in all these years, and each week he came to confession and he did not confess those sins he committed in the jungle, I saw, I knew and I did not say anything because I also saw that he was hurting inside himself and if he would not come back to God, he must forever be hurting inside, and where is he now but hurting even more, now in hell with no one any longer to absolve him."

I absolve you, Manolo! There is me at least to absolve you! Do you hear what I'm saying? I absolve you! Listen and hear me with your soul! There is no evil but in a mind. C! remember when I told you that? remember those nights we talked forever before your conversion? Here it is again! There is no evil but in a mind. Give *me*, Manolo, give *me* your pain! I saw it there, Manolo, in that first story of yours that I began to read, the pain, the thoughts of evil in yourself, and I could not read on because your letter had explained it all, and I took the manuscripts to the fire and I burned them all unread, and I felt then that in burning those papers that I burned with them all the pain of your past and I was in some way releasing even now that suffering that had remained in your mind if not in your body, even when you died.

But what is this I'm saying? What pain? Did I not write but a few pages back that Manolo's death might well have been a happy one, one that he himself had searched for? Am I only looking to bring into myself this suffering that cannot exist any longer for him? There is no evil but in a mind, a little turn of phrase that I write as if it were so astonishingly meaningful. Ha! of course there is evil outside the mind, but wait! wait, if it were only in the mind, does it matter at all? Who is going to tell me what evils pass through my own heart and mind and make them into reality but myself? Look there! over there! at Ihuene examining his penis in a mirror. Are you going to tell him of his evil? He sits just three feet away from me and often he gets up and holds the mirror close to my face and looks at my profile in reflection, comparing it with my own. Then he goes back to watch his penis. Reindude and Michii have been out hunting and have come back with two small monkeys, laughing as they each swing one back and forth. Awaipe and Pendiari are building a second raft, having used their machetes to cut down the balsa trees across the river. They are preparing for our return. Which of you is going to tell them of their evil?

Father Moiseis has not come to say goodbye to the Akaramas. We shook hands when I left the mission this morning, and then he turned and went on his way to plant his corn.

23

It was Yoreitone who first expressed it. "Ooooo-ooooo," he said from some secret depth of himself that had never before been revealed to me, and it sounded like an agony rising from Gehenna, catching us all in its anguish and holding us in fear and terror, a terror we could not understand, for the death itself, the body gone, Darinimbiak being no longer there, had less meaning than the sound emitted by Yoreitone which evoked undreamt of dreams and nightmares, so that I for one floated on waves of fear that tossed me through oceans of Kabbalistic symbols, magic, yearnings. Like one, all of the men of the hut repeated "Ooooo-ooooo, ooooo-ooooo," lifting themselves, drowning themselves, soaring into heavens of exhilaration and wallowing beneath heavy waters that weigh a sea of pain, hallucinating in moans and shakings that gave no respite and continued on throughout a night, set off by that one first tortured lament from Yoreitone, who sat upon his jaguar skin, a god, a priest, a man, and shivered as from cold, while we all circled him, erect but swaying, then bending our heads almost to the earth and coming up again to stare at stars. My moaning emptied me, but what it did to those others around me I cannot say, for we slept all through the following day and then all became normal with the chattering, whispered, visible descriptions of our trip to Piqul, and there were laughter, and demonstrations of machetes, the building of rafts, and days and days it took for talk to stop, and hunting parties again went out and I often with them, bringing back enough to gorge ourselves each time so that I slept and slept, sometimes even inside the hut during the day, where there was so much noise and movement around that at other times would have kept me wakeful.

I live in a world; I live outside it. I live in my pores, in my eyes, my nostrils, ears, mouth, fingers, in all the openings and pulsations of my body. Yet, like the living bundle that did not contain Darinimbiak, I am hollow. I am hollow, vacuous, a vacuum. Being empty myself, my home is now empty. Could I take my brushes and color my insides to suit myself? Could I paint my soul a vivid red, pounding out wavelengths of energy that would light up eyes of men? Or, taking a bit of cadmium yellow light, and with it covering the whole of my mind, would I then burst out a sun? In the night, I rest my head upon the chest of Michii. Instantly, he colors me a color. His hand comes up and brushes my shoulder with orange. Ihuene's thigh settles itself upon my thigh, and a pale violet appears. But these are colors on my skin and I wait and reach for those I long to enter into me. Those days and weeks of years gone by when with brush in hand no color would come to move across the surface of my

stretched canvas, were they the same? Those agonies
when I could not paint and the canvas remained so
blank, and to fill the days, to fill my time, I read a
thousand mysteries and spent endless hours in movie
houses, unthinking, unfeeling, waiting only for the
clock to move ahead, on, on, to when its hands reached
no specified crossing, but without warning suddenly
arrived at a minute of hope and the brush decided it
would cover the blankness and I could laugh and live
again; were they also the same? Is it that I must wait
here for the earth to go on with its revolutions around
itself, to race through space in its orbit until the moment without warning arrives and light itself refracts
through the crystal of my self and colors me with its
spectrum? There is paint again upon my skin, designs that Michii drew there just before we left the
mission, giving me once more the self that he had
known so long, the self who'd learned with him to
shoot an arrow, the self against whom he slept. On our
way, we stood up on our rafts and poled them over
rocks, and ran through jungle with the balsa logs atop
our heads when we came to waterfalls too high to sail
through open air and crash in foam for fun, for Michii
delighted in seeing from what height we could bounce
down and still remain upright. In the evening, when
we beached the rafts, we built fires with matches I
had wrapped in oilskin, and we shot at parrots and
speared for fish, and it was days of childhood, days of
play and love of all things around us. Ihuene, Pendiari, Awaipe, were also caught up in this joy, and we
bumped our rafts together trying to upset one an-

other, a carnival game of twisting with the current, spinning in rushing whirlpools and racing down the center of the river when rocks permitted. There was no world for me but only then that living on that river, it was all, a patch of trees, a patch of sky that followed with us as we moved, and fed us all our needs, and whatever hungers might have pained us were lost beyond our reach, beyond the length of arm to touch them.

Yoreitone sat at the edge of the river with Baaldore awaiting our arrival as if he knew the very moment we would turn the bend from which he first could see us. Our greeting as always was simply "Habe," and since it was then late evening, we went directly into the hut, and Yoreitone sat with us in our compartment and we ate. The earth, the ground beneath me, the place on which I sat, seemed softer, more gentle than I had remembered it; rather, my buttocks seemed to have found a tender spot, for it was there that I had sat so many months, always, in fact, when we talked and ate. The smells inside the hut, the smoke, the fires, all gave me at that moment an overwhelming feeling of belonging, that my body had indeed found not only a place in which to sit, but one in which I had been able and could again and always live in the comfort of my own interior, and had I thought at all then, I would have said or written here, that Yes, Manolo was right, I have found something to carry me through my life.

A stone, Yoreitone sat upon his jaguar skin, unmoving, expressing nothing while he listened as I whisp-

ered out the story of Darinimbiak. At length I told it
and Michii listened, and Baaldore and Ihuene listened, and Pendiari and Awaipe listened as I tried to
repeat the words of Father Moiseis, but never could
give the sense he meant of them, only the horror, my
own horror, yet the dream of Darinimbiak awakened
in all the men of the village, for all had gathered
around, a glow that softened stone; and at the end of
my tale came that terrifying "Ooooo-ooooo" from
Yoreitone, who in nothing more than that single sound
was able to bring a death so close and draw from within
us all spirits that could destroy a soul. And so all of
my own spirits flew out and left me empty, with nothing to carry me through an hour. How much time
must pass now for a hand to rest on mine and bring
with it the sky? How much time before my eyes trans-
mit, transmute the sights on which they focus? Here
in this hot jungle my interior has turned into a winter
landscape, frozen, dried out, stripped of all the foliage
of life. Who? what? will fertilize me now? C! come and
rain on me! Come with paint and water, come and
color up my greys and blacks! That sound of Yoreitone's reverberates within me still. It shook me then,
it cracked me then, as a certain pitch will break a
glass. That's it! You hear? You feel? It comes! Now, it
comes! At this very instant my blood begins to throb
and my hand shakes.

Yoreitone listens:
"There is nothing there in the place of my heart and

intestines where a moon ago lived Darinimbiak. Can you not fill it? I sleep now without his spirit resting on my body. Is he so high in the heights that he cannot see me?"

Yoreitone moans, "Ooooo-ooooo."

"Moons and moons have gone by from the day you sat by me and said, 'You have come a long way and you will rest with us.' Each day since then, I have rested, I have eaten, I have slept, I have hunted and I have laughed. Today, I cannot laugh. You have told me many things because I am ignorant. Today, too, I am ignorant and I cannot laugh for my eyes do not see Darinimbiak and my heart cannot tell me where he is. Can you tell me, Yoreitone?"

Yoreitone grunts, "Oo! oo! oo!"

"Each day we laughed together, and you also came and you laughed with us. Michii laughed and Ihuene and Reindude and Baaldore came and laughed with us, and each day we ate and at night we were all of us together and we lay down one upon the other and we slept. Am I so ignorant that I do not know that Darinimbiak will not again be here with us?"

Yoreitone whispers, "Yes, you are ignorant. And I too am ignorant."

We are naked in the forest.

I had written pages to myself and I needed suddenly again those sounds of Yoreitone, other sounds, so I went to him then, just then when I had put down my pen last evening, and I said to him that I have things I must say. He did not question me, but picked up his jaguar skin and we went out from the hut. I walked close behind that firm, muscular man, as he trod with firm, decisive steps to beneath an ebony tree just off a trail and he spread out the jaguar skin, and he sat on an edge of it and motioned me to sit facing him, also on the skin, and so close we were that our knees touched. And now with his one eye glaring at me, softening with tenderness as he hears my words and feels my gestures, he speaks with words and sounds and with the motion of his flesh, with the motion of his whole body.

"We are ignorant and we stand on earth while there is light and we rest on earth while there is darkness. You are ignorant and you do not know that Darinimbiak is here. His body is not here, but he can live with you in the darkness when you close your eyes. Close them now and he is here. Close them; he is here. I can see him here now. I can hear him. He calls. 'Oooooooooo,' he calls. The moons of his living were not many, not as many as the moons of my living, not as many as yours. He did not live many moons, and it is not good that he has gone to the heights, but his brother went to him in the darkness and called him to the heights and now they are together. That is good. He who placed me in my mother's belly was not ignorant and he told me many things, but he could not tell me all that was inside him because he too went to the heights. Each darkness he looked down on me and spoke to me and told me of his living there, but when Michii came out of a belly, he stopped his speaking and he did not come when I slept. You have not yet made a Michii or a Darinimbiak, and Darinimbiak will come to you until you do."

Has the earth come to my place in its orbit? or is Yoreitone sending into me drop by drop, word by word, touch by touch, the calming emissions of his solitary self with the cadence of his voice, the warmth of his soul? Did he lose an eye so that his remaining one could more easily become a focal point on which to concentrate and thus be hypnotized? My body has begun to rest, the muscles are no longer tense and my thoughts instead of wandering by themselves without control along paths that lead to tangled forests, along paths that trail out from my self in pointless directions, are turning around and now lead themselves to at least the surface of my being. Manolo and Darinimbiak are become one and interchangeable, and as Yoreitone whispers out the name of one, he unknowingly whispers to me also that of the other, and in this darkness that surrounds us under an ebony tree, with black shadows covering us like blankets, this conjuror compels me into a primitive truth that I have known before in other times, that like evil, there is no death but in the mind. Perhaps it is madness now for me to sit within the presence of Yoreitone as he talks of distant heights in which we all will some day live, and see and feel on either side of him the bodies of Manolo and Darinimbiak, come now to laugh and comfort, to show themselves as always living, no ectoplasm floating out from behind a screen, but golems formed with countless particles of the dust of my memories, put together by no magical words or numbers, but by an eye, a shaft of moonlight, a secretion of love, by hands whose fingertips brush on skin that quivers, by arms that wave away the deadly spirits that had come to tempt a soul into its own destruction, by a voice that soothes and liquefies and warms that winter scene.

"It is from the darkness that our spirits come, our good spirits and our bad spirits. They teach us many things and they talk to us and they touch us. And there are spirits that come to fill us with fear. I am ignorant and I do not know why these spirits come, but they have always come, the good spirits, the evil spirits, and we must be content that they are not always evil, and the evil ones do not come with each darkness. Darinimbiak is here and he sees us and he is content."

I sleep, awaken to the sun burning up the treetops, and I am alone upon the jaguar skin. My head is clear and I get up and walk through the jungle to the river and cleanse myself with its ritual waters, and I lie immersed on a bed of sharp rocks. I lie again upon the jaguar skin to dry myself and hunger begins to dizzy me.

24

Once I was a cannibal and it marked a time; death marked another time.

How am I living? What stagnation has set and congealed my unmoving mind? and what becalming influence has shrouded me with this kind of peace that allows no darkness to enter it? My days are days no longer. Time has no thoughts to trouble me, and everything is like nothing and nothing is like everything. For if a day passes, it registers nowhere, and it might be a week, it might be a month. There is no difference. My beard grows and I have it cut. The hair grows on my head and on my chest and groin and it too must be cut. Still, these are growths only suddenly noticed because it prickles me or grates another's skin, and I know then to take my stone and sharpen it and I give it to Michii to do the scraping, for it gives him pleasure. He laughs and comes out with his little gourd of huito and wooden brush, for the scraping away of hair means also the scraping away of paint on areas of my body. Sometimes I look at Michii and think he is older, but then I also think that this is my imagination; for no time can stand still, and though I

may wish that all remain constant, I know that everything changes before my eyes, and I see it, know it, if
only by the length of my hair.

Neither of you out there has aged. Certainly not you
M, for I see you forever as you were and are right now,
working on your latest novel and aching with your
arthritic pains. And you C, you C, what of you? are
you still changing partners or are you living now
alone? Tell me, both of you, from your lives that go
on without me, from your lives that think of me as
dead, eaten by animals, by cannibals, is this really
peace in which I live? Is it happiness? contentment?
What words are there? and why do I ask? What is each
day but a morning at dawn with bodies unlacing, food
and laughter, the noises of everyone awakening and
chattering in whispers, a hunting party of all my
compartment or Michii and I alone, a group outside
the hut sitting and sharpening arrows, or a trip upstream to fish, and hours stretching into darkness and
food again, and finally the interlacing again of our
bodies for warmth, for comfort, for sleep.

I have talked with Hermano, who came like a spirit
from the forest, shocking us all. He arrived one day
with Itaqui, a day that marked another time, and they
were stripped of all their clothing. Hermano was taken
into a compartment while Itaqui slept around the fire,
and they lived and ate there for a little time before
they went away again. For Hermano was in love and
he could not live huddled with men, so close, so far
from her.

It was a day of excitement, for Hermano was looked

upon with awe, the hump upon his back never seen before, another stranger from that other world, all bent over, all different. At first I felt a twinge of jealousy at this intrusion into my isolation, but he spoke to me and I could only love him, feel his need to touch and be so close to Itaqui.

My family was not aware of his presence until he reached the open area of our hut. Nor did I myself know until evening, when I returned from a short hunting trip, and there he and Itaqui stood, naked, unrecognizable to me at first, since they were so far from my thoughts. Nor had I seen either of them before without their clothes. It was not his hump that told me it was Hermano, nor the light color of his skin, but only his face close up, red then with blush as he stood there for the first time in all his life with nothing to cover any part of himself but his hands, which cupped his penis and testicles. He kept looking at the nakedness of Itaqui, who remained apart for only a short time and then was taken up by the women as if they'd known each other always. She held her head high, proud to have come with this odd little man, and she laughed and giggled and embraced the women.

How and why were my questions when everyone had begun to settle down and Hermano and I could talk without so many interruptions. He'd put his shirt and trousers back on and seemed more at ease. "It's nothing short of a miracle that we got here. Only because of Itaqui, who found the food for us and even trapped animals and fish, and we stopped in so many places that she knew of far from here and no one could tell us where you were. It had been in my mind to come to where you were living, but it never seemed possible that we would really arrive." He began to shiver. His face turned white and he put his hand to his mouth and ran to the hole of the hut and crawled out, just in time to throw up all the nervousness of the time since he had left the mission. Baaldore and Michii had followed him and they came back laughing, while Hermano went off to the river to wash.

"Oh, excuse me, señor. Excuse me, but I couldn't help it. All this coming here, the time in the jungle is too much for me. This is the first time I've ever done anything on my own and I don't know that I can stand it. It's too much for me." And he wept and covered his face with his hands. "Where is my Itaqui? Is she going to stay all the time with the women?" I explained our way of life. "Oh," he said, and Yoreitone came over and took Hermano to his compartment, where Itaqui brought him food and he soon went to sleep, shying away from the others, resting his head on the cloth bag he had brought with him full of dried meat and palm shoots.

In the morning, Itaqui again brought him food, which he ate alone, for Yoreitone and the others with whom he had spent the night had already eaten and had gone outside. I had been waiting for him to awaken and had let Michii go off alone, and I went over and sat with him.

"Do you know what it is to live with that man year after year after year?" He began to talk as if at that moment I had asked about Father Moiseis. "Yes, I

know it was my own fault. I could have gone away. I
didn't have to stay with him. But with this thing on
my back, I felt ashamed to go anywhere, to have anyone look at me. Here in the jungle, I felt safe and it
was in a way good for me because I was always able to
feel superior to the Indians. I come from the mountains and I am educated and I can read and write.
I've seen things they had never even dreamed existed
and I know how to cook in a frying pan, I can turn on
a radio or a victrola, I have clothes. I don't paint myself and I know Christ and God. How can they com-
pare to me? They must look up to me and admire me.
They are nothing but savages, even those who have
been at the mission for years. They have never seen
Cuzco, and I have been to so many places. Or so I
thought until I talked and listened to Manolo and
made friends with Itaqui. She taught me more than any
books I've read. She might still be a savage, but she
knows me now and maybe in her own way she loves
me. It is nice to think that she does. At least she stays
with me and goes wherever I say and does what I tell
her to do. And now here, in this place, I cannot sleep
next to her. Can you know what it is to go through a
whole life as empty as mine and suddenly to find love?
Manolo gave me that. How could I have lived those
years as I did? It came to me one day not long ago that
it is not only my own fault, this way that I lived, but
also the fault of the padre. Manolo led my thinking in
this direction and I could see then that the padre came
and took me with him when I was just a child, a horror
to look at, and he told me it was God's will that I am

so ugly and that I suffer so much, and that I must be godly myself so that I will go to heaven when I die. Sometimes he looked at me and turned away in disgust, and sometimes he would look at me with pain on his face as if he himself were carrying this on his back. But all the time he gave me food and a place to sleep and I helped him at every mission we went to. Loving Itaqui has made me different somehow. It is almost as if I don't any longer feel my hump. At night when she touches me, it seems flat and smooth and I can't tell whether or not it is still there. And no one laughs at me any more. Even if I am ugly and crippled, it doesn't mean that I don't know how to love someone, does it?"

He got up then and I thought he would cry again, but instead he smiled and he went out in search of Itaqui, who had gone with the women to gather peanuts. The following evening he said he could not stay with us, that he needed the body of Itaqui next to him at night, and if she agreed, they would go the next day, but to where he did not know. And so Hermano has again disappeared from my life, leaving me my days, my nights, my pleasures.

25

"Fill the emptiness!"

Those words of Yoreitone's come back to me now
with such clarity and meaning for myself as if always
before my coming here I had searched for some filling,
as if there had been within me such a vast emptiness
that my whole being, my whole physical self and my
soul, were together in search of some region then not
known to me, perhaps a people, a manner of living
with hardship, primitive ways; as if for some reason
primitive life, I don't know how, but somehow could,
not wash me of what had passed for my life within
civilization, but could enter and flow through my veins
with a new kind of blood that would circulate
throughout my system and pump new energies
through my heart; in all the emptiness of my days and
years there had never been anything that touched my
soul that had in any way compared with my past wanderings, wanderings in areas difficult to survive. How
often did I empty the little there was within me onto a
stretch of canvas, and the hollowness that followed
echoed with unsatisfying pain at each knock of that
fate that I then demanded. Did you, did anyone then

sit on the soul of my sounding board, rapping in search of solidity, finding only that emptiness? Did you, in all the years of my life, see me as I was then, as I must always be, nothing more than a seeker? I came into a jungle to live a new incarnation, and now discover that I am more a part of the family of Man than a part only of those men with whom I spent such days and nights of love? It is not possible, for I have seen it, felt it, lived it, denied it, dreaded it, it is not possible for, oh! I know it now, to step out of the skin I've worn for most all my life and grow or put on a new one. I am a cannibal, but I am no savage, for I cannot swallow my paint and allow it to color me inside as I will it, as I had thought I might turn back my own time and live as Michii with his mind. The color remains outside me, used with brush to spread my uncertain life across whatever material appears before me, and I begin to see things now with all my past and all my present mixed together, unsorted as they may be, confused and intermingled, with importance and without, but all of pieces that strangely fit together and I learn only now, or maybe I always knew it but only now can I sense its truth in everyday reality, I learn that my self is made of all my selves, not only of the parts I wish to show, the parts that can be seen from outside, but there is also that interior that so often cries my agony and denies me all my rights, denies me all the things I also am, the same interior that forces me along these paths of forest that lead me toward a Darinimbiak, a Father Moiseis, a Manolo, and a Michii, the same interior without which I could not have come and loved and secured myself, to replace within me some of that past loneliness that I could hardly bear, again, a loneliness without which I could never even have made a picture on a canvas.

A time alone, only a few weeks ago, with the jungle alive and vibrant around me, and Michii and Baaldore gone with all the other men to hunt, I saw within myself too many seeds that would grow a fungus around my brain, encasing it with mold that could penetrate and smooth the convolutions and there I would remain, not he who had traveled and arrived, not the me who had crossed the mountains in a search, but another me living only in ease and pleasure, no longer able to scrawl out words on paper or think beyond a moment. And days later, I took myself up from our hut, and I walked on again alone without a word to any of my friends and family, but left when all again were gone and I walked through my jungle and passed the mission from a distance thinking, Are you there, Father Moiseis? Are you older now, more alone and sad than ever? Are you still teaching your people your ways they will not understand? and I say to myself, No, that's not for me, it isn't me who would live that way, to stay and stultify and try to change a life, I'm made of sterner stuff, and if Manolo said it all, he said it also of myself, and passing there where none had seen me, it was if I'd skipped a step into my future and I saw an instant ahead of me where time again was moving with hands upon the faces of clocks and there was no reaction of horror or fear of return, but nothing more than a quicker breathing and I looked again upon your faces and to myself I smiled and thought, Oh let them weep for me alive.

I took a walk alone and I carried with me all my back would take of food, and here I am now back at my beginning in Pasñiquti, sitting on a hard bed as soft as softest feathers, writing under netting made for mosquitos and vampire bats, having eaten a piece of home-grown cow I cut with knife and fork, and bread spread with cold butter, beer I drank that came from Holland, and I sat on a chair and leaned my elbows on a table. Here there are unfamiliar noises, half-forgotten, grating chairs, a creaking bed, a dish inside a sink, the humming of a tune, all bringing me back so slowly, but so surely. I walked alone, and naked I walked inside this door that has a handle, works on hinges, has a key to turn a lock. I did not blush and hide myself when men in clothes stared, and shrank back, and when I told them who I was, there was a shock of recognition and a fear of me at first, a strange, wild man with faded paint on his nude body, looking like any savage, though none had dared before to come to this place, but then with clean face, with trousers, shirt and shoes to cover me, all borrowed articles, they offered me beer and food and talk and listened quietly to my tale.

A growth of beard had covered my face when I arrived, for I went unshaven those days of walking, days without Michii to cut away the hair of my body, days so different from those long ago days of my departure from this very place when I exhilarated with each step toward the mission, going out to look for the same self that I always was. Even at myself I can smile now, as Manolo must have smiled when we first met and he looked at me with his own past of wandering and searching, sometimes also finding. Now again I cannot answer questions, but at this moment there is no need because I go where my legs will take me and if I look ahead, it seems like time gone by, for I see myself no matter where I go, forever here.